"This book is food for the min___
faith, politics, and policy will be____
shared by Leith and Galen."

—TIM PAWLENTY, Governor of Minnesota (2003-11)

"The apostle Paul reminds us to 'pray for kings and all those in authority, that we may live peaceful and quiet lives in all godliness and holiness.' Leith Anderson and Galen Carey offer a practical reminder that as believers, we have the privilege of letting the timeless truths of Scripture guide our decisions as we select those leaders and vote on the issues."

—JIM DALY, President, Focus on the Family

"Biblically informed voting among followers of Jesus is far too rare today. *Faith in the Voting Booth* by Anderson and Carey provides a valuable resource for anyone who wants to cast their vote in a manner consistent with Scripture. Carefully consider its contents and then prayerfully cast your vote."

—PAUL NYQUIST, Ph.D., President, Moody Bible Institute

"As those who are charged to be the salt of the earth and the light of the world, Christians have both a moral and spiritual imperative to vote. Part of influencing the flavor, feeling, look, and tone of our nation and indeed our world is accomplished through the prayerful and thoughtful casting of ballots at our local voting booths.

"It is with this in mind that Leith Anderson and Galen Carey's book, *Faith in the Voting Booth,* is such a timely work. From the very practical matter of registering to vote to the provision of a biblical framework through which to analyze some of the hot button issues of our day, they offer a very helpful tool for any Christian who desires to honor his/her dual citizenship at the voting booth."

—CLAUDE ALEXANDER, Pastor of
The Park Church, Charlotte, NC

"The right book for a pivotal moment. Leith Anderson and Galen Carey have done a great service with this thoughtful, articulate guide. Combining religion and politics can be explosive, but Anderson and Carey offer wisdom and leadership. They are an example of how Christian faith should engage political action."

–RICHARD STEARNS, President, World Vision U.S.,
and author of *The Hole in Our Gospel* and *Unfinished*

"The most comprehensive, thoughtful, and researched book ever written on living out our faith as we vote. This is NOT just some simplistic 'Voter's Guide.' This falls in the category of Discipleship as a witness for Christ. The reading is compelling and rich in both biblical and historical narratives that impact our thinking both domestically and globally now and in the future. The course of history could be changed.... Take the challenge!"

–JO ANNE LYON, General Superintendent
of The Wesleyan Church

Faith in the
VOTING BOOTH

Faith in the
VOTING BOOTH

LEITH ANDERSON AND GALEN CAREY

ZONDERVAN

Faith in the Voting Booth
Copyright © 2016 by Leith Anderson and Galen Carey

Requests for information should be addressed to:
Zondervan, 3900 *Sparks Dr. SE, Grand Rapids, Michigan* 49546

ISBN: 978-0-310-34610-4 (ebook)

Library of Congress Cataloging-in-Publication Data

Names: Anderson, Leith, 1944-
Title: Faith in the voting booth / Leith Anderson and Galen Carey.
Description: Grand Rapids : Zondervan, 2016. | Includes bibliographical references and
    index.
Identifiers: LCCN 2015039654 | ISBN 9780310346098 (softcover : alk. paper)
Subjects: LCSH: Voting—Religious aspects—Christianity. | Christianity and politics—
    United States. | Christians—Political activity—United States.
Classification: LCC BR516 .A54 2016 | DDC 261.70973—dc23 LC record available at
    http://lccn.loc.gov/2015039654

Unless otherwise noted, Scripture quotations are taken from The Holy Bible, New
International Version®, NIV®. Copyright © 1973, 1978, 1984, 2011 by Biblica, Inc.® Used
by permission of Zondervan. All rights reserved worldwide. www.Zondervan.com. The
"NIV" and "New International Version" are trademarks registered in the United States
Patent and Trademark Office by Biblica, Inc.®

Scripture quotations marked ESV are from the *ESV*® Bible (*The Holy Bible, English
Standard Version*®). Copyright © 2001 by Crossway, a publishing ministry of Good News
Publishers. Used by permission. All rights reserved.

Scriptures marked KJV are from the King James Version. Public domain.

Scripture quotations marked (NLT) are taken from the *Holy Bible,* New Living
Translation. © 1996, 2004, 2007, 2013 by Tyndale House Foundation. Used by permission
of Tyndale House Publishers, Inc., Carol Stream, Illinois 60188. All rights reserved.

The views and words of this book are those of Leith Anderson and Galen Carey and
should not be construed or reported as the positions or policies of the National
Association of Evangelicals or of any other organizations past and present with which
Anderson or Carey has been affiliated.

Any Internet addresses (websites, blogs, etc.) and telephone numbers in this book are
offered as a resource. They are not intended in any way to be or imply an endorsement
by Zondervan, nor does Zondervan vouch for the content of these sites and numbers for
the life of this book.

Cover design: *Faceout Studio / Jeff Miller*
Cover photo: *Blend Images / Hill Street Studios / Getty Images*®
Interior design: *Kait Lamphere*

First printing January 2016 / Printed in the United States of America

CONTENTS

Chapter 1

WHY WE WROTE THIS BOOK

"Never discuss religion or politics in polite company." This book discusses both.

Religion and politics are at the bedrock of human society. Sometimes they have accomplished breathtaking good, and sometimes they have perpetrated unspeakable evil. But keeping quiet won't make either one go away. Both are here to stay. The United States is a political democracy with lots of religious people.

In May 2015 the Pew Research Center released the results of a survey asking more than 36,000 American adults (ages eighteen and older) about their religious affiliation. Christians are the largest group with 70.6%; non-Christian faiths combine together into 5.9%; 22.8% say they are unaffiliated; and a tiny 0.6% claim they don't know or refused to answer. At the top of their analysis of these numbers the Pew researchers wrote, "To be sure, the United States remains home to more Christians than any other country in the world, and a large majority of Americans—roughly seven-in-ten—continue to identify with some branch of the Christian faith."[1]

Compare religious affiliations to Americans' political affiliations. When asked which major political party they belong to, 23% say they are Republicans, 32% identify as Democrats, and 39% claim to be independents.[2] Deeper questioning shows that most of those independents clearly tilt toward one political party or the other even though they don't want to declare alignment with either.

However, political affiliations and leanings don't all turn into votes on election days. The United States may be the oldest continuous democracy in the world, but that doesn't mean that we all vote. Typically our nation reports a 40% turnout for midterm elections and a 60% turnout of eligible voters for presidential elections. That puts the United States far behind democracies like Australia, Belgium, and Chile with compulsory voting that reaches around 90% and also less than such voluntary voting nations as Austria, Sweden, and Italy that near 80%.[3]

While we know that some self-identified Christians, Jews, and Muslims never show up at their church, synagogue, or mosque and that some self-identified Republicans and Democrats never register or vote, most do both. The big picture is that the United States is a nation of citizens who are religious and who vote. Since our faith and politics are deeply connected in our thoughts, relationships, and communities, they are important to think and talk about. We should want our faith to inform and influence our politics and ballots.

WHO IS THIS BOOK FOR?

Every reader is welcome even though not every reader may agree on every point in the book. Certainly there are universal values and principles for all, but we have special audiences in mind on just about every page.

If you are a Christian, an American citizen who wants to vote wisely and well in local, state, and national elections, this book is for you. If you don't describe yourself as an "evangelical," don't stop reading. This book can still be for you. There is frequent misunderstanding in the use of the word *evangelical*, and you may be surprised that a term you don't like actually describes you better than you expected. At least read chapter 4 about "Christians and Evangelicals."

If you are a thoughtful person who wants to decide for yourself about both faith and politics rather than being told what to believe and how to vote by someone who wants to decide for you, this book is for you. You know that television ads, social media blasts, and political posters are designed to do your thinking for you. You live a busy life and don't have the time you would like to listen to speeches and debates, read long articles and books, or try to balance competing cable television commentators. You are reading this book to get some direction on how to figure out how to vote without being told who to vote for. You are open to ideas, especially if they come from the Bible, but you want to think for yourself and decide for yourself.

If you welcome teaching from the Bible and want to pray for God's direction before sending a check, endorsing a candidate, or casting a vote, this book is for you.

WHO ARE THE AUTHORS?

You wisely want to know something about our faith and politics, the names behind the words.

Both of us—Leith Anderson and Galen Carey—are leaders of the National Association of Evangelicals (NAE) headquartered in Washington, DC. The NAE was founded in 1942 to form a national network of organizations and individuals who believe in Jesus Christ and take the Bible seriously. The purpose of the association is to honor God by connecting and representing evangelical Christians. Today the NAE serves millions of Christians in forty denominations and a long list of churches, colleges, universities, seminaries, missions, publishers, businesses, and individuals. Ministries include World Relief (international relief and development agency), Chaplains Commission (endorsing military chaplains for the Army, Navy, Air Force, and Veterans Association), and departments serving and connecting to the global church, the American church, and our country's government.[4]

It's important to know that the NAE is not a political organization, doesn't endorse candidates, and doesn't align with any political party. Think of the NAE as a national team of committed Christians who start with God, the Bible, and the church and then reach out to be an influence for good everywhere possible from churches and campuses to Congress and courts.

Leith Anderson is currently the president of the NAE, a position he has held since 2006. He also served as a longtime pastor of two churches in Colorado and Minnesota. He earned degrees from secular and religious schools, has written many books on the church and Christian faith, has been married to Charleen since he was twenty, is the father of four adult children, doesn't live and has never lived near Washington, DC, and has never endorsed a political candidate or told others who he is voting for.

Galen Carey became the vice president of the NAE for government relations in 2009. Galen grew up in the Philippines, where his parents were missionaries, and he has carried that calling into relief and development ministries in Chicago, Croatia, Mozambique, Kenya, Indonesia, and Burundi. He and his wife, Delia, and their two sons have loved and cared for the poor and vulnerable around the world. Galen has learned how to get by in many languages, but is fluent in both Spanish and English. Most of his work now centers in Washington, where he is well known and connected to members of Congress, White House staff, and dozens of faith-based and other organizations in the nation's capital.

WHAT NOT TO EXPECT

Want to know who to vote for? Want a list of criticisms and attacks on politicians we don't like? Want a definitive advocacy for policies and candidates of school boards, planning commissions, city councils, county judges, state legislators, governors, members of Congress, and the White House? This book will do "none of the above."

Our desire is not to tell you how to vote. And we hope you don't want us to tell you how to vote. What this book is about is describing how to decide for yourself.

Don't expect every issue to be addressed. Actually, don't expect *most* issues to be addressed. There will be critics and advocates for important causes who will be sure to say, "They didn't say enough about …" or "They completely left out…." They'll be right. Short books in a generation of rapidly emerging and changing moral and political challenges will be sure to overlook a lot.

WHAT TO EXPECT

Look for biblical emphasis. We seek to introduce biblical teaching and thought as the starting point for political decisions and engagement. Expect content that is thoughtful and respectful—acknowledging the diversity and sometimes divisive differences among Christians and showing respect to all. Anticipate content that is nonpartisan—avoiding identification with and endorsement of any political party or platform. And expect a book that is durable—not just about one election cycle, but relevant to future elections and politics.

Half of the chapters deal with specific issues including poverty, diversity, marriage and families, immigration, taxes, prisons, foreign policy, and creation care. They are all major topics in the opening decades of the twenty-first century. They are given as examples of how Christians can understand these issues and apply the Bible to addressing them. In some of these chapters the perspectives of the authors come through. This is not to tell the reader what to think or how to vote, but to acknowledge that we have easily researchable positions seeking care for the poor and desire for reform of America's immigration and incarceration systems.

IMPORTANT!

Most people in most of the world for most of history have had no power in politics. They couldn't vote for their representatives or choose which wars to fight or taxes to pay. Most people have been and still are poor, vulnerable, and oppressed. Most people couldn't imagine reading a book about how to connect politics with their faith other than to pray for God's help.

The faith and politics of the United States of America is often referred to as the "American Experiment." That may seem like a strange description for a form of government that has lasted more than two centuries. The truth is, we are still a young nation, and our future is neither known nor guaranteed. What and how we believe as Christians and vote as citizens is crucially important. We have both privilege and responsibility; we should cherish the privilege and fulfill the responsibility.

Remember that most Americans in the past did not have the privileges and responsibilities of faith and politics that are ours. Once upon a time in the United States, the voting booth was open only to free men who owned land. As never before, we are the land of the free, and that freedom includes how we vote. This is a book about believing and voting.

Chapter 2

HOW TO VOTE

Prior to every national election, organizations on the right and left and in-between distribute "voting guides" basically telling you how to vote. We won't be doing that. Instead, we will start by explaining how you actually cast your vote. It may seem easy, but if you have never voted in an election, it could be daunting. Since less than half of the population of the United States turns out for elections, it's safe to assume you may have never voted. For you, this will be "Voting 101," for veteran voters, a refresher course.

And while we will not ask you to vote for any particular candidate or ballot initiative, we *will* tell you how to vote. But our most important message? Vote!

Most Americans would probably like to believe that voter turnout in our democracy leads the world. Far from it. The top nations, all with over 90 percent, include Australia, Austria, Belgium, and Italy. Percentages tend to run higher in Western Europe and Canada than in the United States (around 50 percent with higher rates in presidential election years than in other election years).[1]

Analysts study and debate why so many Americans don't vote, but all should agree that those who do vote wield large influence through the ballots they cast. Yet so many citizens of our democracy have surrendered their voices. Why don't Americans vote?

- *"My vote doesn't matter."* Believing that one vote won't make much difference or that the electorate is so favorable toward

15

a candidate a voter doesn't like or a party a voter disagrees with leads to apathy and discouragement.

- *"People like me don't much vote."* Some groups are much more likely to vote than others. Less likely to vote are Asians, Latinos, younger men, and people with lower income. More likely to vote are whites, African Americans, older men, and people earning more than $150,000 per year.

- *"Not this time. Maybe next time."* Voter turnout is much higher in presidential election years or when major offices or issues are on the ballots. Primary elections, midterm elections, and elections that are perceived as less important attract fewer voters.

- *"I just don't know."* Some of us don't vote because we don't know how to do it or can't figure out who to vote for. So we just don't try.

- *"I've got my reasons."* Personal reasons include disinterest, busyness, anger against government, lack of transportation, and forgetting.

A FEW BASICS

Qualifications for voting in the United States include U.S. citizenship, being at least eighteen years old by Election Day, established residency where voting, and being registered by the deadline, if there is one. Some states have variations and limitations such as government photo IDs and other requirements. These seem like simple qualifications, but they become more complicated for the homeless, Americans who live overseas, and others with special circumstances. In the past, the United States significantly limited or excluded from voting Americans who were women or minorities and those who didn't own land. Some states currently disqualify those who have been convicted of a felony crime even after they have completed their sentences.

You can find out if you meet voter qualifications by doing some research online—a good place to start is https://www.usa.gov/register-to-vote. You may also call or visit your local government center (city hall, county courthouse, state capital building, etc.).

Most elections are held in the spring or fall, but local elections can be called for just about any time to fill vacancies, pass school bonds, or change taxes. Presidential elections are always held on the Tuesday after the first Monday of November. (The earliest possible date is November 2, and the latest possible date is November 8.) Presidents are elected every four years, senators every six years, and members of the U.S. House of Representatives every two years. State and local elections often align with federal election dates, but can be scheduled at any time allowed by state and local laws. Many states offer early voting, and all offer absentee ballots for those who cannot come to the polls on Election Day.

Voters may choose to sign up as members of a political party. In some states this allows them to participate in caucuses where smaller groups of party members gather to discuss their party's political views and choose who will be supported by their party.

Primary elections are held to choose which candidates will represent the political party in the coming general election. Membership in a political party may be required to vote in a primary election, although in some states voters may sign up just before that election.

General elections are open to all qualified voters and make the final decision on who is elected or how a government law will be decided (taxes, amending the state constitution, deciding on a referendum, etc.). After the general election, the votes are counted and the winners are announced. Usually there is a time lapse of a few months before the winners actually start the official duties to which they have been elected.

All this may sound technical and confusing to a first-timer, but government officials, neighbors, and friends are usually glad to walk someone through the process. Once you have voted, it gets easier to understand and more comfortable the next time.

SIGNING UP AND SHOWING UP

The two primary actions for voting in the United States are signing up to vote and showing up to vote. Some rules on how to do both vary by states and communities. While the basic process is similar across the country, it's a good idea to check out the specifics in your own hometown. Here is what to do:

1. **Check qualifications.** Go through the qualification checklist and call city hall with any questions.

2. **Find out if you are registered.** Some states allow registering to vote when getting a driver's license, so some voters may already be registered and not know it. Check with city hall.

3. **Register to vote.** Voter registration is usually required in advance of voting—maybe thirty days or more.

   City hall is the place to go, or look up online "Voter Registration" with the state's name. Some states, like Minnesota, allow voter registration on Election Day at the poll. But every state is different, and registration should be researched and handled in advance. Typically, once you have registered and remain living at your current address, you do not have to register again.

4. **Find out where to vote.** Voting locations are often in schools, church buildings, or other public buildings. Most towns have multiple locations, but you have to vote at the right one near your home, so asking in advance is important.

5. **Get a sample ballot.** Sample ballots will be just like the ballots on Election Day. The easiest way to get a sample ballot is online at the town website. You can then print it for review and practice. This preparation makes voting a whole lot easier.

6. **Research candidates and issues.** Checking out all the choices may take some time, but makes for smarter decisions. There is no requirement to vote on everything, so any voter is free to skip parts.

7. **Show up on Election Day.** Go to the nearest polling place and get in line to vote. In major elections there may be a wait. Earlier in the day works best for many people. Absentee ballots are available for those who will be away or otherwise can't show up on the actual Election Day. Some states and towns require a good reason, and others allow any registered voter to vote in advance.

   Absentee ballots must always be submitted or mailed before the actual Election Day; advance time limits are usually longer for citizens living overseas and shorter for citizens residing in the United States. Some states also have an early in-person voting period of several days or weeks, allowing voters to go to a central location to vote in advance.

8. **Complete the ballot.** When your turn comes, you will be shown into a booth with a curtain, where you can mark your ballot. Or, in some places you move switches on a

19

machine or have an electronic or other system to cast your votes. Either way, privacy is always provided. Volunteers are nearby to answer questions and to show voters how to work the voting system. Special provisions are available for voters with disabilities.

All ballots are added up after the end of voting on Election Day, and the results are announced on television, radio, the Internet, and newspapers. This reporting may take only a few hours, but complications can delay announcements of winners. In some unusual cases technical problems, tie votes, or other issues may trigger recounts and even occasional repeat elections—but these situations are relatively rare.

Chapter 3

WHO TO VOTE FOR

You may think the "how to do it" is the easy part. Or, "I knew all that … so just tell me who to vote for." As we promised from the outset, we will not tell you who to vote for. That is your personal responsibility. But we will offer some guidance on how to make those decisions:

1. RESEARCH

Take time and do the work to be informed about issues and candidates. It's not possible to learn everything, but use available tools (television, radio, Internet, newspapers, magazines, and conversations with helpful, knowledgeable persons) to know enough to evaluate what advocates are saying. Keep asking questions—and research the answers as if God is going to give you a quiz.

Remember that there is a surplus of false or heavily slanted information available. Never rely on a single source.

2. BEWARE

Many good and godly candidates and supporters are transparent and tell the truth. Sadly, too many are neither transparent nor truthful. We don't need to be cynical, but we should keep up our guard and beware of television ads, political brochures, partisan blogs, newspaper opinions, and social media pressures.

Money has become a powerful political tool. Consultants decide how best to influence potential voters and spend billions of dollars to convince potential voters. Negative advertising can be powerfully influential even though it is distorted and biased.

3. CONSIDER

Consider which candidates best align with your values and will govern for the greatest good. Character, experience, policies, and promises are all part of the consideration.

Most voters like to choose a candidate who is like them. Veterans like veterans. Union members like union members. Athletes like athletes. Republicans like Republicans. Democrats like Democrats. Christians like Christians. It's normal and often good to choose a candidate who is similar, because that person may best represent you. But sometimes this approach doesn't work. Athletes who are good at their game may be poor politicians. And devout Christians may not always make wise government decisions. So consider these characteristics, but don't let identity be the deciding factor.

4. COUNSEL

The counsel from people we trust—friends, family, pastors, church members, neighbors, Bible study group partners—can help us decide how to vote. They are all helpful for learning and choosing. Always allow the greatest influence to come from those who are godly, competent, and knowledgeable.

One way to think about where we get our counsel is to ask

whom we would choose to disciple us in our Christian faith, be named the executor of our wills, or counsel us in a crisis.

5. PRACTICE

A helpful and practical procedure for any important life decision can be used in deciding how to vote.

- Choose who to vote for.
- Write down your choice.
- Pray daily for God to confirm the choice or not.
- Without telling anyone, live with your choice for a week or more.
- If convinced and comfortable, stick with the choice when voting.
- If unconvinced and uncomfortable, change the choice and repeat the process.

6. PRAY

"If any of you lacks wisdom, you should ask God, who gives generously to all without finding fault, and it will be given to you" (James 1:5).

When the New Testament was written, there was no democracy, and the idea of political voting probably never crossed any Christian's mind. But they did know a lot about facing "trials of many kinds" (James 1:2) and needing divine wisdom to figure out what to do. James wrote that they should pray and ask God for wisdom to make the right choices. This is where we begin our journey to voting choices: we admit that we need help and ask God for direction.

There is always a temptation to first make up our minds and then pray for our choices to be implemented by God. That's not the Christian way. We begin with submission to the mind of Christ and the will of God and ask for divine influence on how to vote. Start now—pray daily for wisdom. Be open to divine surprises.

7. LOOK TO THE BIBLE

The Bible is God's book that is designed to deliver the wisdom we pray for in all areas of life, including deciding how to vote. "You have known the Holy Scriptures, which are able to make you wise for salvation through faith in Christ Jesus. All Scripture is God-breathed and is useful for teaching, rebuking, correcting and training in righteousness" (2 Tim. 3:15–16).

A repeated theme in this book is to start with the Bible and apply the Bible in making political choices. This may not make sense to non-Christians, but it is our priority as followers of Jesus. On some topics, such as poverty, the Bible has extensive specific directions. On all topics the Bible is the foundation for our values, thinking, and actions—even on topics about which the Bible does not specifically speak. When tempted and pressured by politicians and their advocates, keep going back to the Word of God to see what it has to say. And pray that you will interpret politics by the Bible rather than interpret the Bible by politics.

8. DECIDE

Now it's time to decide. Make the choice. Commit the decision to God. Trust God that your choice is what it should be and that God will use it for good. Get ready to turn the choice into your vote.

Imagine Jesus with you in the voting booth asking, "How did you decide?" and know that you have a good answer to explain your decision.

9. VOTE

On Election Day, go to your polling place and cast your vote. Be grateful for the right to vote and confident that you did your best to be a good Christian steward and a wise American citizen.

10. KEEP PRAYING

As you walk away from the voting booth on Election Day, keep praying. Ask God to use your vote and the votes of others to accomplish his purposes in our nation. Pray for God's blessing on whoever is elected, even if they are not those for whom you voted. Tell God you believe he is sovereign and you will trust him to use the election for good.

11. FOLLOW UP

We live out our Christian values regardless of who wins or loses. We share these values with others, including those who are not Christians. We may help the poor, love the immigrant, care for

God's creation, pay our taxes, support strong marriages, speak for the unborn, promote religious freedom, show respect to those who are different, seek justice for those in prison, and advocate for all created in God's image within politics and outside politics. This is more than an election cycle involvement; this is a Christian lifestyle.

Voting is not the end. It isn't even the beginning. The Bible doesn't specifically mention voting or tell us to vote. Voting is simply one expression of living out our Christian faith in loyalty to Jesus Christ and in conformity with the teaching of the Bible.

Follow-up can influence the votes of others and can insist on accountability for elected officials to keep the promises they made when elected.

FAITH AND COURAGE

John F. Kennedy won a Pulitzer Prize for his bestselling 1957 book *Profiles in Courage*. The book tells the stories of eight U.S. senators, most before the Civil War, who took stands and cast votes that helped shape America and save the Union. Most of their names are now unfamiliar. Many of them suffered political losses and defeats for doing what they were convinced was right. They brought careful thought and political courage to American government.

We face serious challenges that require courageous leaders who are willing to look beyond the next election and seek the long-term health of the nation. We need leaders who will focus on governing, not thinking about how to get reelected. By voting for candidates who are statespersons, not just politicians, we support leaders who will be the next profiles in courage.

How we vote demonstrates our faith and courage. As Christians, everything begins with our commitment to Jesus Christ as Savior and Lord. As Christians, we seek to live and vote with the Bible as our guide for belief and behavior. Then our faith joins with our courage to vote for candidates and policies that will bless others rather than just ourselves.

We are God's agents to help shape America for good. Be faithful. Be courageous.

Vote.

Chapter 4

CHRISTIANS AND EVANGELICALS

That evangelicals are Christians "who take the Bible seriously and believe in Jesus Christ as Savior and Lord"[1] was the very short description in a 2015 speech Leith gave at a Washington, DC, conference sponsored by the American Association for the Advancement of Science. After the speech several Roman Catholic priests came over to say thanks for the definition and said, "That means we also are evangelicals."

Many Catholics, members of mainline Protestant denominations, and independent Christians who are outside evangelical groups claim to be "evangelicals." It is a term embraced by many you would not expect and avoided by many who are evangelicals.

When reading research and reviewing polling, you may be surprised to discover that different research organizations use different definitions and then end up with conflicting reports.[2] Some say that evangelicals are "born-again Christians." Some choose to define evangelicals as church members in denominations belonging to the National Association of Evangelicals and a few other denominations the researchers have added on. One angle is to ask, "Do you believe in a literal interpretation of the Bible?" even though many evangelicals would answer the question with another question, "What do you mean by literal?" Another popular approach is to ask, "Are you an evangelical?"—and if the answer is "yes," then that person must be an evangelical, and if the answer is "no," then that person must not be an evangelical.

Depending on which definition or identification is used, the numbers of evangelicals range from around 10 percent to about 40 percent of the American population. At a time when many followers of Jesus like to avoid labels, it's hard to know which definitions actually work.

LET'S GET A WORKING DEFINITION

In the academic world studying religion and politics, David Bebbington has become an international authority in defining and describing who evangelical Christians are. His writing is especially helpful, because he gives a list of characteristics that reach around the world and not just the United States. He is a professor of history at the University of Stirling in Scotland and a fellow of the Royal Historical Society, and he has an American connection as an adjunct professor at Truett Seminary of Baylor University in Waco, Texas. Bebbington lists four convictions that identify evangelicals:

1. Conversion—having a "born again" experience that brings eternal new life to a person who believes in Jesus as Savior

2. Action—turning faith into practice with evangelism and social action

3. Bible—believing and obeying the Bible as top authority

4. Cross—conviction that Jesus died on the cross to provide salvation from sin[3]

Would all evangelical Christians be able to pass a quiz on these four characteristics? Probably not. But this list helps us get a sense of who evangelicals are, what they believe, and how they want to live out the Christian faith.

Confusion arises both inside and outside of evangelicalism when large groups of Christians identify with all four of these characteristics but aren't sure they want to be called evangelicals. These groups range from some Southern Baptists to some African-Americans to Catholics to Christians in independent churches that aren't aligned with any denomination. This reluctance to be labeled as evangelicals may come from a desire for another primary identification like those who say, "I'm simply a Christian and that's all the description I want or need," or "Just call me Lutheran," or "I'm a Pentecostal and I think that's different from being an evangelical. But I can't tell you what the difference really is." However, a big reason why many avoid the term is because they think it is too much of a political label that doesn't describe them.

DOES "EVANGELICAL" MEAN "POLITICAL"?

Does "evangelical" mean "political"? The short answer is "no," but it takes some explaining.

There is a myth that evangelicals are white and Republican and live in the suburbs. Yes, this describes some evangelicals, but overlooks evangelical African Americans, the growing number of Hispanic evangelicals, and millions more who are not in churches belonging to evangelical denominations. Plus, some American denominations have the word *evangelical* in their name but don't think of themselves as evangelicals according to the Bebbington description. And, you are right, this can get confusing!

Start with some common sense. The World Evangelical Alliance (WEA) has its roots in 1846 and its official organization in 1951. Today, the WEA claims to represent 600 million evangelicals in 129 countries.[4] Are most of these hundreds of millions Republicans or white? Overwhelmingly, they are neither. Most of them live outside of the United States and know little or nothing about American political parties, elections, laws, or politics. They have nothing to do with our political system, and many of them have little or no power in their own country's politics. Yet they are evangelicals for sure.

The big point here is that evangelicalism is centered in faith and not in politics. We should be very cautious when connecting the term *evangelical* (which comes from the New Testament Greek word *evangel*, meaning "good news") with politics. Individuals and groups who are evangelical have dramatically different political interests, speak different languages, and live in countries around the globe.

Does this mean evangelicals should never be connected with politics? Of course it does not. People from many political parties and ideologies have targeted and persuaded evangelicals to join their platforms. Some evangelicals have targeted and monopolized political philosophies, organizations, and candidates. Most of all, there is a long and well-documented history of evangelical "activism" (one of Bebbington's four characteristics) that has rallied evangelicals to found universities, denounce slavery, oppose abortion-on-demand, and take other initiatives that have brought them into the political arena. When rightly done, evangelical activism begins with evangelism and justice and not with politics. Faith leads to politics and not the other way around.

Because "evangelical" is so often portrayed as a political identity by the national press, it can be difficult to convince outsiders that politics aren't primary.

A few years ago my wife, Charleen, and I (Leith) signed up for a new experience—a three-day cruise out of Fort Lauderdale to Mexico and back for about $275 each. The first night aboard the ship, we went to an assigned dinner table, and someone asked for everyone at the table to introduce themselves and tell why they were on this trip. The woman next to us said she took the trip to get some rest because she had spent the past year as a political activist trying to stop evangelicals from taking over the country. She said, "All those evangelicals really scare me." Then it was my turn. It just didn't seem like a good idea to introduce myself as "President of the National Association of Evangelicals." The problem was that she saw evangelicals totally in terms of politics and not in terms of faith.

To evangelicals, faith comes first. Taking the Bible seriously and believing in Jesus as Savior and Lord is more important than any politics. Politics and everything else flow out of faith and come much later in priority.

LOTS OF DIVERSITY

There aren't many differences among evangelicals when it comes to conversion, action, the Bible, and the cross. That's because someone has stepped outside of the defining circle of evangelicalism if they don't want to be "born again," live out their faith, and acknowledge the authority of the Bible and the conviction that Jesus died on the cross to provide human salvation. But not all evangelicals are faithful and consistent in all they affirm. Evangelicals fail far too often, exercise faith that is far too small, and are sinners who don't always live up to their beliefs. But this is who evangelical Christians are. Even though there is no central organization or universal church hierarchy to enforce evangelical belief and practice, these four characteristics are clear and unifying.

Once this central core is set, there are endless varieties, expressions, and beliefs in evangelical communities. Some baptize babies, some baptize only adults, and some don't baptize at all. Some speak in tongues; some forbid speaking in tongues. Some have ordained clergy; some avoid ordained clergy. Some emphasize free will; some emphasize predestination. Some serve wine for communion; some serve grape juice. Some have women pastors; some forbid women pastors. The expressions make a very long list, but all are built around the consistent core of being evangelicals.

When it comes to race, ethnicity, language, and social class, the diversity is so broad that it can be hard to track. Many of the largest evangelical churches in America are Hispanic, African-American, Korean, Hmong, Chinese, and more. Certainly evangelicals have significantly risen in socioeconomic status over the past half century, but many evangelicals are poor and working class. Evangelical churches are common in rural towns, inner cities, and metropolitan suburbs. To describe or identify American evangelicals as limited to one race, one class, one language, or some states of the nation is to significantly misunderstand evangelical Americans.

Add political leanings to the list of diversities. While evangelical African Americans and Hispanics tend to be Democrats and white evangelical southerners tend to be Republicans, there are millions of exceptions to these stereotypes. When you sit these different evangelicals around a table, they are sometimes surprised by the political differences but simultaneously comfortable with their common faith in Jesus and the Bible.

WHO'S IN CHARGE?

Catholics know that the pope is the head of the Roman church. Mormons know that their headquarters are in Salt Lake City. Tibetan Buddhists all look to the Dalai Lama. But who is in charge of evangelicals, and where are their headquarters?

The answer is that evangelicals have no official human leader and no headquarters.

Evangelicals are highly decentralized. Unlike others in the most traditional Protestant and Catholic traditions with hierarchies and headquarters, evangelicals have very little of either. Evangelicals have colleges, universities, publishing houses, denominations, tens of thousands of churches, and millions of people—but no centralized control or voice. Just as anyone can have a business card saying "Consultant," anyone can self-describe as an evangelical Christian. This can become embarrassing when a self-appointed pastor in a self-organized church makes the news with bizarre beliefs and behavior and is then described as an evangelical by the pastor or the press. Even when this is offensive and obviously untrue, the pastor and the press can still do it and often get away with it.

Evangelicalism is about Christian faith. Evangelicalism is a movement. Evangelicalism is a set of basic beliefs and behaviors. Usually evangelicalism is good. Sometimes it is dysfunctional.

Most evangelicals are ordinary Americans who belong to local churches that are affiliated with national denominations and networks. Many of the best-known denominations are members of the National Association of Evangelicals—credible, healthy, normal. But no leader or organization is the boss of evangelicals.

Chapter 5

CHRISTIANS AND POLITICS: DO THEY MIX?

Galen's first exposure to politics was a stint as a poll watcher in Chicago. That city is known for its political corruption, but there have always been reformers trying to clean things up. As an idealistic young seminary student, Galen volunteered to be a poll watcher. He was excited to be able to help end political corruption and usher in a new era of electoral justice.

At 5:00 a.m. on Election Day, Galen arrived at the assigned polling place, eager to get to work. The precinct captain took a look at his papers and gruffly told him that he wasn't needed and that he should go to another precinct halfway across the city. After some hesitation, Galen stood his ground and was allowed to stay. By 8:00 a.m. he had made so many calls reporting violations that the reform group had to tell him just to focus on the major issues. It was quite a day!

Hearing stories like this, many Christians conclude that politics is a dirty business, filled with greedy people seeking to get rich at our expense and maybe take away our rights in the process. When urged to "throw the rascals out," they respond with a hearty "Amen!" They readily forward chain emails with preposterous distortions about our national leaders.

Others see politics as a way to "take back our country." Troubled by moral decay and economic malaise, they long for a return to biblical values. Electing godly leaders would seem to be a first step toward this end. As we walk the halls of Congress and meet with our nation's leaders on behalf of the National Association of Evangelicals, we find that many are discouraged and privately acknowledge their disillusionment with public service. As one senator put it, "I didn't come to Washington to sit around doing nothing. I came here to serve the people, to get things done." Another, a passionate advocate for human rights in forgotten corners of Africa, confided that the voters back home didn't seem to care. He lost his reelection bid.

The Bible tells us that rulers are in power because God put them there: "For there is no authority except that which God has established. The authorities that exist have been established by God" (Rom. 13:1). We are admonished to pray for them (1 Tim. 2:1–2). Sometimes we do, but usually only for those with whom we agree. We often disrespect the rest in our private speech and even publicly in our blogs, tweets, articles, and online commentary.

Many Christians just disengage. In a recent person-on-the-street survey of civics literacy, only one in seven respondents knew the name of the current vice president.[1]

How should Christians approach politics? Does the Bible offer any usable guidance? Will God tell us whom to vote for? Does our vote even matter? And is politics only about voting?

BIBLICAL GUIDANCE

The Bible presents complex and seemingly contradictory messages about government. It is God's servant for the common good, as Paul explains in Romans 13. But it is also a blasphemous beast that persecutes Christians, as John vividly portrays in Revelation 13.[2] Most of the time, it is a little of both. Paul and John both wrote in the context of the Roman Empire—which sometimes protected Paul as a Roman citizen but eventually executed him.

No particular system of government is prescribed by the Bible for all times and places. Believers are never directly commanded to participate in politics or to abstain. Instead, the Bible offers us wisdom that we then attempt to apply to political questions.

In Genesis, for example, we find the story of God making a great nation from the descendants of one human couple, Abraham and Sarah (Gen. 12:1–3). Abraham and his tribe had to make treaties and negotiate conflicts with neighboring tribes and eventually seek protection and survival under a pagan Egyptian empire that later enslaved them.

Through Moses, God liberated the Israelites and gave them the Ten Commandments, as well as detailed laws covering the political, economic, and religious life of the nation.[3] These laws were designed for a particular nation with a unique mission, but they offer insight into how people can live together under God, giving special care to the most vulnerable members of the community.

Even with "good legislation," the Israelites under Moses complained, rebelled, and worshiped idols. When told to engage in battle, they cowered in fear. When told not to take any loot for themselves, they hid it in their tents. Moses had to plead with God not to destroy the people. Sometimes in politics the problem is with the citizens, not just their leaders.

Israelite governance evolved over the centuries from nomadic tribal chiefs, through a long period of slavery, to charismatic judges and culminated with a series of kings and prophets.

The kings were mostly disappointing, though some were better than others. Does this sound familiar? But the ideal political leader is well summarized in Psalm 72, a hymn that is either by or about King Solomon, while ultimately pointing to the promised Messiah. The king was to rule with and embody justice and righteousness, fostering prosperity for all and paying particular attention to the needs of the poor. The king was to be benevolent, but powerful; he was expected to take on, and even crush the oppressor. We would do well to have more Psalm 72 leaders in our day.

The historical books, such as 1 and 2 Samuel and 1 and 2 Kings, present a candid account of how far short Israel's very human kings fell from the royal ideal. We are taken into the back rooms of the palace, where we sometimes find nobility and spiritual fervor, but more often intrigue, power plays, corruption, oppression, immorality, and even idolatry. These sins eventually meet with God's judgment via conquest by neighboring tribes and distant empires. Modern-day political scandals shouldn't surprise us.

Even as the Israelites languished in exile, secular governments were used by God to bless the people. Some of our Old Testament heroes served these governments in prominent roles. Joseph developed a forward-looking food security program for Egypt and its neighbors. Nehemiah, Daniel, Esther, and others pursued honorable careers in the administration of vast empires. Their service blessed the people. Even pagan rulers carried out God's purposes. Jeremiah called King Nebuchadnezzar "God's servant" (Jer. 25:9), and Isaiah referred to King Cyrus as "God's anointed" (Isa. 45:1). An effective leader doesn't necessarily have to share our religious beliefs.

The biblical prophets confirmed both the majestic vision of God's gracious reign and the travesty that human governance too often made of God's provisions. When government fell short of its divine calling, the prophets did not call the people to withdraw from public life. They called the people to spiritual renewal, to fasting, to hearing God's word, and to caring for the needy. Ordinary citizens in Old Testament times did not have a vote, but they did have a moral claim on their leaders' stewardship of the responsibilities of office. The quality of the people's lives before God influenced the well-being of the nation (for example, 2 Chron. 7:13–14). This raises an interesting question: Is the way you live consistent with the way you vote?

The New Testament offers various views of government, some quite positive. An imperial decree helped fulfill biblical prophecies related to Jesus' birth (Luke 2:1). The gospel writers were surprisingly respectful of the Roman occupiers. Jesus praised the faith of a Roman centurion as being greater than what he found among the Jews (Matt. 8:10). At Jesus' death it was another Roman centurion who first recognized Jesus as the "Son of God" (Mark 15:39). Of course, this same centurion had participated, along with Pilate, in the crucifixion of Jesus on trumped-up charges (Matt. 27:12–14).

Government leaders are, in Paul's words, full-time ministers who serve both God and the people (Rom. 13:1–7). The governing authorities have many responsibilities: They not only prevent and punish violations of the public trust, but also provide public goods and reward citizens who contribute to the common good. Christians are called to obey their rulers as part of their submission to God.[4]

But we also see King Herod murdering babies and his son, Herod, beheading John the Baptist. We see Caiaphas and Pilate conspiring to crucify Jesus. We see certain local authorities jailing and whipping Christians and seeking to stamp out the Christian movement. And we see the abuse of power chillingly unmasked in John's apocalyptic visions in the book of Revelation.

From the wisdom of the Bible we learn that government is an instrument of God for our good, but it can be corrupted and become a tool of evil, even satanic oppression. We also discover that believers who participate even in corrupt, secular governments can be used by God to bless the world. And unbelieving leaders can help to fulfill God's purposes for our nation.

Others are appointed prophetically to call the nation to

repentance. The prophetic role is critical. As longtime former Zambian President Kenneth Kaunda once said, "What a nation needs more than anything else is not a Christian ruler in the palace, but a Christian prophet within earshot."[5]

WISDOM FROM HISTORY

In addition to the Bible, we can look to history for clues about how we should engage with politics and government. Through the centuries Christians have held different attitudes toward government and responsible civic engagement. Some Christians withdrew from the broader society into monasteries, but they quickly discovered the importance of effective internal governance. They inevitably found themselves in need of commercial, political, and security arrangements with their neighbors. In modern times, the Amish have been remarkably successful in maintaining a countercultural community, but even they have to negotiate with the broader society on such issues as traffic safety and education policy. It took a 1972 Supreme Court decision, *Wisconsin v. Yoder*, to establish the community's right to not send their children to high school.[6]

Other Christians, following the Emperor Constantine, have sought to Christianize government and enlist state power to ensure that God's will is done "on earth as it is in heaven." This approach paved the way for the institutional spread of Christianity, but also produced false conversions, hypocrisy, and other unintended consequences. Those who want government to enforce right behavior forget that even God allows the wheat and tares to grow together until the harvest (Matt. 13:24–30).

Neither approach—withdrawal or domination—does full justice to biblical teaching, and neither has been vindicated by the historical record.

The political participation of American evangelicals has varied significantly over our history. Evangelicals actively supported many of the great social reform movements of the nineteenth century—including, notably, the abolition of slavery, women's suffrage, and the temperance movement. Although the fundamentalist-modernist controversies in the early twentieth century led to a period of withdrawal, leaders such as Carl F. H. Henry were instrumental in reawakening evangelical social concern.[7]

Concern about the excesses of the sexual revolution and the general moral decay of American society drew some evangelicals into alliances with Catholics and political conservatives that collectively came to be known as the Religious Right.[8] Other groups focused on social justice and peace and aligned more often with liberal politics. While differing on the substance of many issues, these groups and others like them agreed that Christian faith requires direct engagement in political life.

In 2004 the National Association of Evangelicals adopted "For the Health of the Nation" as a platform for evangelical civic engagement.[9] It presents a way of thinking biblically about government and politics and outlines a balanced agenda with seven areas of common concern that evangelicals from across the political spectrum and doctrinal divides can support: religious freedom, family, sanctity of life, poverty, human rights, peace, and care of God's creation.

POLITICS AND POLITICAL PARTIES

The nature of responsible participation in political life will vary according to context. Christians in North Korea, for example, have few political options, but they can still live in a way that shines light into the darkness—sometimes at great personal risk. Christians in the United States, by contrast, have a wide range of options and corresponding responsibilities.

For most of our history, the United States has had two major political parties. That remains true today, although Gallup reports an upward trend of 43 percent of Americans who now identify as political independents.[10] This is partly due to a general disillusionment with leaders who seem more interested in fighting each other than in finding ways to work together. But it also reflects a growing concern among many voters that neither party represents their interests and concerns.

The goal of a political party is to gain control of the government and use that power to advance the interests of party members. That sounds self-serving, and often it is. But political parties offer a way for like-minded voters to collaborate and maximize their impact. Some Christians will be called to work within party structures to pursue their vision for just governance. *Partisanship* does not have to be a dirty word, so long as its practitioners keep a sense of perspective. Working in a political party involves both cooperation and competition—internally and externally. We just have to remember that our allegiance to God and his kingdom comes first.

As we work on elections, supporting candidates and their political goals, let's remember that our biblical faith goes much deeper than politics. As we gather to worship the King of kings and Lord of lords, our political differences with those who worship alongside us pale into insignificance.[11]

Given the remarkable privilege of having a voice in the selection of local, state, and national leaders, it is surprising that so many Americans do not take advantage of this opportunity. In some cases this is a matter of disillusionment with the choices presented, or the belief that one's vote doesn't really count or isn't important. Schools also share in the responsibility. Many students graduate from high school with little or no education in civics and public affairs. One is reminded of the quip by Winston Churchill, who reportedly lamented that "the best argument against democracy is a five-minute conversation with the average voter."[12]

INCREASING THE IMPACT OF OUR VOTES

Voting, of course, is only one aspect of political engagement. We can follow up by keeping in touch with our elected leaders and holding them accountable to keep their promises. Personal meetings with officials or their staff or handwritten letters are particularly effective.

When we meet with elected officials in Washington to discuss issues of concern to the National Association of Evangelicals, we usually receive a respectful hearing. But politicians are most responsive—and rightfully so—to the constituents they directly represent, those who will have the opportunity to vote them in or out of office in the next election. Citizens can multiply the impact of their vote by keeping their leaders informed of their concerns on specific topics.

A particularly creative approach has been developed by Bread for the World, a network of Christians working to end hunger and poverty. Churches are encouraged to hold an "Offering of Letters" in which parishioners write letters encouraging their leaders to take specific steps on behalf of poor and hungry people. The letters are collected in offering baskets, enabling participants to symbolically offer God the gift of their citizenship as well as their money. The letters are then mailed to the appropriate members of Congress.[13]

Most churches and nonprofit organizations agree that it is unwise to engage in partisan political activities or to use their mailing lists or facilities to benefit particular candidates. But they can certainly engage in nonpartisan voter registration, mobilization efforts, or education on the issues.[14]

While most Christians will engage in political life as laypeople whose major focus lies elsewhere, some should consider careers in government or public service as politicians, pollsters, policy advisors, or administrators. Others can educate voters and influence public opinion through careers in print and broadcast journalism, think tanks, and advocacy groups.

Also important is having committed Christians in the worlds of arts and entertainment, where culture and values that influence politics are shaped. As the British evangelical abolitionist William Wilberforce came to realize, after struggling for years to get Parliament to pass a bill banning the slave trade, culture is upstream from politics.[15] While we may not always get the government we deserve, as some claim, we usually get a government that reflects the values of our culture and society.

HELPING EVERYONE TO VOTE

We have made considerable progress since the days when only free male landowners were allowed to vote. We sometimes forget that this progress was only achieved at great cost and with much struggle. And there are still barriers that prevent some citizens from voting. Some states have laws preventing those who have committed felonies from ever voting again, even after they have completed their sentences and have reentered society.

Since the U.S. Supreme Court invalidated parts of the Voting Rights Act in *Shelby County v. Holder*,[16] some states have passed laws reducing absentee voting periods and requiring voters to show identification at the time they register or when they vote. Supporters say these changes will reduce the incidence of voter fraud. But critics claim they are aimed at discouraging certain voters from participating. They argue that there is scant evidence of voter fraud and that the laws disproportionately impact low-income and minority voters.

DOES MY VOTE MATTER?

On rare occasions, elections have been decided by a single vote.[17] However, the Christian's vote matters not because it decides an election, but because it is an act of faithful stewardship of our citizenship. Voting is an act of Christian witness. Voter participation increases the legitimacy of elections, and thus the mandate of those elected. Voting puts politicians on notice that we care enough to participate. Even if our vote does not decide the outcome of a particular election, it is still needed. If we think others should vote, then we should vote, too.

George O. Wood, General Superintendent of the Assemblies of God, put it well in a challenge to greater civic engagement by members of the denomination:

> You are privileged citizens of a blessed nation. Use your citizenship well! Seek the common good. Advocate for the last, the lost, and the least. Speak the truth in love. And vote for candidates and issues that reflect a biblical perspective on issues. The difference in so many conflicts in American politics and culture turns on who turns out to vote.[18]

Chapter 6

PRINCIPLES AND PRIORITIES

Evangelical and Jewish leaders meet annually to share our biblical roots and discuss our distinctive religious beliefs. In a small-group discussion at a recent gathering, a rabbi mentioned the disturbing 2012 ruling of a court in Cologne, Germany, banning male circumcision.

The ruling triggered months of debate across Germany and in the Bundestag, the German parliament. Medical experts and legal scholars sided with different political parties and proposals. One piece of draft legislation would have forbidden all circumcisions below the age of fourteen and then only with the boy's informed consent after the age of fourteen. This would have made illegal the millennia-old Jewish practice of circumcising boys when they are eight days old. The political debate included "acrimony, frostiness and at times brutal intolerance," according to Dieter Graumann, head of the Central Council of Jews in Germany.

Eventually, on December 12, 2012, the Bundestag voted 434 to 100 to grant parents the authority to have their sons circumcised by a trained practitioner.[1]

Let's imagine that we are devout Jews in modern Germany who are deciding which candidate to support in an upcoming election. One of our choices is a politician from our hometown who belongs to the same political party we have joined and who supports almost all of our values and political preferences. Friends say that he is a good businessman and will be a strong advocate in the Bundestag. However, this otherwise desirable candidate strongly opposes circumcision and wants to make it illegal in Germany. Should we Jews vote for this candidate?

Probably our vote will go to another candidate even though the other candidate belongs to a different political party and supports policies that are deeply disliked. Why? Because male infant circumcision goes back to the covenant when ninety-nine-year-old Abraham was himself circumcised along with every male in his household "as God told him" (Gen. 17:23–24). Circumcision is at the central core of Jewish faith, tradition, and identity. It is a higher priority than political parties, national budgets, immigration policies, or the qualifications of a candidate running for office.

EVERY VOTER PRIORITIZES

When we go to our polling places, our ballots may offer only a few candidates. But those candidates represent positions on hundreds—maybe even thousands—of issues. Some issues are trivial and temporary; some are influential and irreversible. We are not just voting for a candidate, but for all of the issues that candidate claims to support. With so many issues in politics and government, it's almost impossible to fully understand them and their impact on our communities and nation. The best we can do is to identify the ones that matter the most to us and then try to assess which candidate will support those issues.

This process of selecting the most important issues that will influence our vote is hard enough, but finding a political candidate who exactly aligns with our list is usually impossible. Some candidates don't even align with their own lists; they agree to support platforms they don't agree with in order to gain a nomination, party support, and their names on the ballot. And even when we think we have a close match between our political beliefs and the candidates of our choosing, we may be disappointed if the person we voted for changes positions once elected.

All of this means that voting is not an exact science and that uncomfortable concessions are often necessary. For example, you might consider voting for a candidate based on his or her opposition to abortion. But what if that candidate's views on other issues do not align with what you believe to be a biblical worldview? Some Christians would adamantly argue that we should ignore all those other issues and support only pro-life candidates. Then there are other Christians who are party loyalists, who check off on the ballot the party that they think is most "Christian." Others believe they should only vote for fellow Christians who share their faith.

The list goes on to include voters who always pick the incumbent or always vote against the incumbent. There are even some voters who so dislike the ballot candidates that they write in names ranging from relatives to pets as a form of political protest. In each of these examples (some good and others not so good), a prioritization has taken place and has guided the voter to a selection.

PRINCIPAL PRINCIPLES

It is easy to say, "My Christian faith determines my priorities when it comes to voting." But what does that mean? How does that work? We offer the following, knowing that you may want to reorder this list or just create your own. Either way, start with principles and then move to political choices (and then double-check the choices to make sure they are consistent with your principles).

1. **The Bible gives guidance.**

   The Bible is God's inspired and authoritative Word and is therefore our rule for faith and practice, including political practices and votes.

2. **Our highest loyalty goes to Jesus.**

   Jesus Christ is our Savior and Lord. Our highest loyalty as Christians is as followers of Jesus. Our commitment to Jesus is ahead of our commitment to our country, our families, ourselves, and all others.

3. **God created his image in everyone.**

   The image of God is created into every human being from conception until death and into eternity. Therefore we must always treat every person and support policies with recognition of God's image and with dignity and respect that honors God.

4. **Love God and neighbor.**

   As followers of Jesus we believe that "God so loved the world that he gave his one and only Son, that whoever believes in him shall not perish but have eternal life" (John 3:16).

   We are called by Jesus to love God and others as God loves us. Jesus said, "'Love the Lord your God with all your heart and with all your soul and with all your mind.' This is the first and greatest commandment. And the second is like it: 'Love your neighbor as yourself'" (Matt. 22:37–39). Jesus gave special attention to our neighbors who are most vulnerable and suffering.

5. **Sin pervades our world and politics.**

   Don't be surprised by sin—it's everywhere. Sin is everything contrary to divine law. It is anything that is wrong rather than right. The premise of the gospel is that we are all sinners and that Jesus came to save us from all the sin in our world and in our lives, and from all the present and eternal consequences of human sin. So when sin shows up in politics and government, we are not surprised but we are reminded why we need and believe in the good news of Jesus Christ. Christians are not called to despair, but to be agents of God and "salt and light" in our world so that others "may see your good deeds and praise your Father in heaven" (Matt. 5:13–16).

6. **Choose justice, mercy, and humility.**

God has called us to turn right beliefs into righteous actions. The prophet Micah in the eighth century BC gave a profound answer to a top question: "He has showed you, O man, what is good. And what does the LORD require of you? To act justly and to love mercy and to walk humbly with your God" (Mic. 6:8).

7. **Uphold the standard of righteousness.**

Righteousness is an eternal attribute of God. When righteousness is our standard, we seek to do everything God's way. The difference between right and wrong is not determined by public opinion, human culture, or personal preference. Our standard is summarized in 1 Peter 3:6: "Do what is right and do not give way to fear."

8. **Pursue the common good for all.**

Christians have long shown compassion for others, following the teaching of Jesus in the parable of the good Samaritan that calls his followers to "Go and do likewise" (Luke 10:37) to others as the Samaritan did for the man who was mugged. While the ethical concept of common good has sometimes been abused, the Christian principle is to seek the best for everyone and not just for ourselves.[2]

9. **Trust God no matter what.**

Christians have often been persecuted and even martyred without experiencing the outcomes for which they have prayed and lived. As those who truly believe that "in all things God works for the good of those who love him, who have been called according to his purpose" (Rom. 8:28), we are committed to trust God even when politics seem to be going in the wrong direction.

10. **Be responsible.**

Whether Christian or non-Christian, ethicists teach that morality and responsibility go hand in hand. We must not only believe what is right and know what is good; we are also responsible to use our God-given resources to *do* what is right and good. "Anyone, then, who knows the good he ought to do and doesn't do it, it is sin for them" (James 4:17). We abandon our personal responsibility with the expectation that others will do that which is good on our behalf. This extends to paying taxes, voting in elections, and helping the poor and vulnerable. None of us can do everything, but we are responsible to do our part.

11. **Religious freedom rises to a high value.**

Religious freedom allows individuals and communities to believe, worship, and practice their faith as they choose without control or coercion by any government. It includes the freedom to change from one religion to another. The Roman Empire allowed greater religious freedom than most ancient nations, and that helped Christianity to sink roots and grow. In America, religious freedom is guaranteed by the First Amendment to the U.S. Constitution, although threats and restrictions are growing as popular trends conflict with religious beliefs.

12. **Be practical and realistic.**

Because we live in a democracy that encompasses millions of differences, we can't always get what we believe is good and right. That's certainly the way it was in Israel during the life of Jesus. The Romans imposed severe and often immoral laws on the Hebrew people. Then and now we are required to accept some trade-offs, join coalitions, and work with those who disagree. Holding onto and advancing our convictions in a democracy full of differences is and will continue to be a huge challenge.

13. **Obey the law, most of the time.**

Romans 13:1–7 tells Christians to obey government officials and pay taxes. We are to do this with respect and honor. These must have been hard words to read when the Roman emperor was torturing and killing Christians and when fellow believers were being sold into the atrocities of slavery. The principle is to obey the law but recognize that this is not an absolute principle. If a human law is unjust or immoral, it may be necessary to disobey it in order to obey God's higher laws.

14. **Pray for government leaders.**

Unbelievers may speak severe and ugly words toward politicians, but Christians are to be best known for the way we pray for our government leaders—even the ones we don't like, the ones we disagree with, and the ones who want to harm us. Paul's first-century exhortation equally applies to twenty-first-century Christians in America: "I urge, then, first of all, that petitions, prayers, intercession and thanksgiving be made for all people—for kings and all those in authority, that we may live peaceful and quiet lives in all godliness and holiness" (1 Tim. 2:1–2).

PICK PRIORITIES

Priority is an interesting word because it came into the English language as always singular.[3] It means "first," and only one item can top any list. Apparently the word stayed singular for 500 years until our culture decided that there can be many first things.

Let's go back to the earlier definition. When thinking about political importance, what is number one on the list? Suppose the choices include Democrats, Republicans, taxes, abortion, marriage, immigration, climate change, national defense, and religious freedom. Which one comes first?

This is a hard question. We live in a democracy where we expect to have plenty of priorities. We insist that they are all important. And they are all important ... even though they may not be equally important. Let's make the question even harder: On a list of top ten priorities, which nine should be surrendered in order to win what is the most important?

The good news is that most Americans can have multiple priorities. The disappointing news is that most of us won't ever get all we want. We must decide what is more important and what is less important.

BACK WHEN POLITICS WERE BAD

Politics couldn't have been much worse for Israel in the sixth century BC. The city of Jerusalem, including the temple, was besieged and destroyed by the Babylonians, and thousands were forced to relocate to Babylon. If we asked what those captive Jews held as their highest priority, they probably would have answered, "To go home." That makes sense to us. Probably exactly what we all would have wanted. Instead,

This is what the LORD Almighty, the God of Israel, says to all those I carried into exile from Jerusalem to Babylon: "Build houses and settle down; plant gardens and eat what they produce. Marry and have sons and daughters; find wives for your sons and give your daughters in marriage, so that they too may have sons and daughters. Increase in numbers there; do not decrease. Also seek the peace and prosperity of the city to which I have carried you into exile. Pray to the LORD for it, because if it prospers, you too will prosper" (Jer. 29:4–7).

These words from the prophet Jeremiah may have dumbfounded the Israelites. They were told to settle in and prosper the pagan capital city of their enemies who defeated them in war, destroyed their homes, and ruined their place of worship. Plus, God claimed to be behind their defeat and captivity.

Some of the Israelites' own prophets encouraged them to pray and push for their return to Jerusalem. But God's priority was different. He wanted them to stay put in the land of their enemies for seventy years and prosper in place. He also wanted them to ignore the leaders calling them home: "Yes, this is what the LORD Almighty, the God of Israel, says: 'Do not let the prophets and diviners among you deceive you. Do not listen to the dreams you encourage them to have. They are prophesying lies to you in my name. I have not sent them,' declares the LORD" (Jer. 29:8-9).

God's priorities weren't what the Israelites expected. The same prioritization applies to us. For example, we may agree that we should get a tax break for contributing to the church. But what if God's goal is to teach us to tithe without getting a tax deduction, and America goes to a flat tax with no charitable deductions? After all, most governments aren't as generous as the United States on this. A flat tax could be hard on already tight budgets and maybe it will never happen. But the point is that we prioritize God's commands over our preferences.

Not all of the Israelites' sixth-century BC principles were the same as our list of fourteen, but many overlap. Giving priority to staying put in a place they never would have chosen aligns with the principles to love God and neighbor, uphold the standard of righteousness, pursue the common good for all, trust God no matter what, be responsible, be practical, be realistic, and obey the law most of the time (even the laws of a pagan conqueror).

In this story of personal and political prioritization comes one of the Bible verses frequently quoted by evangelical Christians: "'For I know the plans I have for you,' declares the LORD, 'plans to prosper you and not to harm you, plans to give you hope and a future'" (Jer. 29:11).

Make a list of your top ten political preferences—if you could get everyone and everything you want (candidates, issues, political party, etc.). Check your list against the principles list. Arrange your preferences in order of importance. Start at the top of your list and work your way down, knowing that you may need to eliminate some of the lower items to get the more important ones at the top of the list.

Chapter 7

WHERE MOST EVANGELICALS AGREE MOST OF THE TIME

Where do Americans agree? With so much polarized politics, the frequent comment is that "we agree to disagree." Except that many don't even agree with that.

We don't need to list the disagreements among our nation's millions of citizens, but we should note that there are topics on which most of us agree most of the time. National Public Radio developed a short list of points with 90 percent-plus agreement. "I would say that 90 percent plus is pretty close to full agreement, given the normal 'noise' that we find in polls, wherein there is never 100% agreement with anything," according to Frank Newport, editor-in-chief of The Gallup Poll.

More than 90 percent of Americans believe in God or in some form of universal power. More than 90 percent of Americans believe that future generations should be prepared for the ramifications of living in a global society. More than 90 percent are proud of the members of the U.S. military who served in Iraq. More than 90 percent of Americans agree that the development of good math skills is essential to success in life.[1] Add it all up, and most of us believe in some form of God, the world, veterans, and math. Sort of. But this doesn't seem like much, does it?

WHAT ABOUT EVANGELICAL CHRISTIANS?

American evangelical Christians also have their disagreements. Similar to the rest of the population, we evangelicals represent a range of generational, racial, ethnic, gender, socioeconomic, geographic, and denominational differences. But we have broad consensus on key issues that inform and shape our votes. To understand the common ground of evangelical agreement, it's helpful first to learn about a few myths.

MYTH: ALL EVANGELICALS THINK AND VOTE ALIKE

Political analysts often talk about evangelicals as if we all agree on most issues, like all the same candidates, and will cast similar votes on Election Day. The analysts do this for multiple reasons— because they have heard it from others; because they've read a poll that reports the politics of a plurality or majority, and they round off the results to the nearest 100 percent; or because most people like generalizations that put large numbers of differing people into the same category.

We can tell you from thousands of conversations over years of experience that evangelicals are politically conservative, liberal, Republican, Democratic, and independent. While it is true that polls report most white suburban evangelicals are conservative and vote Republican, they should add that most African-American evangelicals are likely to vote Democratic and that most Hispanic evangelicals are conservative but also tend to vote Democratic.

An interesting exercise is to visit six evangelical churches on six consecutive Sundays and listen to how many talk about politics in sermons or in hallway conversations. It doesn't take long to learn that Christians are far more likely to be discussing Jesus, the Bible, church, children, jobs, and football than talking about politics.

Evangelical churches and parishioners are Christians first and surprisingly unpolitical.

MYTH: EXCEPTIONS PREDICT THE FUTURE

Some self-appointed prophets like to find exceptions and use them to describe the future. Popular predictions foresee declines in church attendance, new sexual attitudes, and shifting worship music styles based on the preferences of current eighteen-to-twenty-four-year-olds. Even though the researchers have based their predictions on a limited sample of a specific generation, they want us to assume that this is what the future will bring. Just a few minutes of Internet research reveals multiple lists and documentation of past religious and political predictions that didn't come true.[2] Dangerous are the prophets who have a personal preference on what they want the future to be and then have made their predictions to fulfill their dreams or to advance their causes.

None of us are guaranteed prophets. Predictions often miss their mark. Doomsayers aren't always right. Hopeful idealists can get it wrong.

This is not to say that thoughtful analysis of trends cannot be very helpful. Rather, we should be slow to believe everything we see on the Internet, hear from a speech, or read in a magazine or book.

MYTH: ANALYSTS ALL KNOW WHAT THEY ARE TALKING ABOUT

An email came to my (Leith's) inbox showing a photo of an anti-American billboard posted in a midwestern city by Muslims. The text of the email used the photo as the basis for an analysis of Islam in America and a warning of a frightening future for Christians. But it just didn't seem right or make sense to me, so I did some checking. My research showed that the billboard never existed. Instead, some anonymous zealot Photoshopped the picture to create a particular view of Islam. Totally made up. So I carefully replied to the original email and reported my research. I also suggested that the sender contact everyone who had been sent the original photo and commentary to tell them that the billboard never existed.

Because there are tens of millions of evangelical Christians with computers in America, it is not surprising that thousands of independent analysts are posting their ideas as thousands more trust all they say. Many—possibly most—of these analysts offer helpful, legitimate commentary on a variety of issues important to Christians. But don't believe everything you read on the Internet, especially those alarming messages with the requisite "pass this along to all your friends." Check them out for yourself to decide if they know what they are talking about. Be wary of random emails that warn of impending doom. Look to reliable Christian leaders to see if they are offering similar warnings. Consult your pastor. You might also consider websites that specialize in debunking Internet myths, such as www.snopes.com, www.breakthechain.org, and www.truthorfiction.com.

This myth extends to preachers, websites, mass mailings, and especially the millions of paid radio, television, and social media ads that populate the airwaves in election years. The difference with paid political ads is that the professional messages may be intentionally incomplete or misleading. Again, approach these messages with a healthy skepticism and check them against other sources before you accept them as truth.

MYTH: DIFFERENCES MEAN DISAGREEMENT

We are tempted to imagine that all differences grow from basic disagreement. Often we have fundamental agreement on what we want, but differences on how to get there. For example, some Christian voters strongly favor homeschooling or private parochial schools, and other Christian voters strongly favor public schools. These are real differences, but both views are founded on a deep, biblical desire to raise godly well-educated girls and boys. The profound underlying agreement is greater than the differences over educational policy.

So where do we as evangelicals agree? What beliefs do we hold in common that should not be ignored because of a focus on surface differences?

AGREEMENT ON THE BIBLE

Evangelicals agree that the Bible comes from God and provides a standard for what we believe and how we live. This belief may seem to work for true believers, but triggers frequent misunderstanding in others.

When the Bible is quoted to explain beliefs about sexual morality, marriage, raising children, paying taxes, or treating immigrants, critics often come back with counterarguments that go like these: "How can you believe the Bible when it commands capital punishment for religious offenses?" or "The Bible endorses slavery, and nobody believes that anymore, so why believe anything else the Bible says?" or "The Bible forbids divorce, and you Christians get divorced like everyone else, so what difference does it make if you ignore other Bible rules?"

Often these critics really don't know what the Bible actually says. Looking up the words under discussion in the Bible and reading them in context is a good place to begin.

It is helpful to understand that the Bible has levels of laws just as the United States has levels of laws. In our country there are infractions (like traffic tickets), misdemeanors (like simple assault), and felonies (like bank robbery or murder). We even have multiple layers within these three categories, including, for example, gross misdemeanors, manslaughter, and premeditated murder. In the same way, the Old Testament distinguishes between minor rules such as requiring parapets to be constructed on roofs to prevent people from falling off (Deut. 22:8) and major rules such as the sixth commandment, "Thou shalt not kill" (Ex. 20:13 KJV).

As with American laws, the Bible has levels of laws related to killing another person ranging from self-defense, home protection, and unintentional manslaughter, to premeditated murder. As we read the Bible, we discover that its laws shaped our laws, that a serious look makes more sense than a superficial reading, and that many of the caricatures are neither fair nor legitimate. It is also important to distinguish between the Old Testament's civil and ceremonial laws for the nation of Israel and the Bible's major and universal moral laws.

Old Testament divorce laws provided protection for women in centuries when women were often mistreated. Agriculture laws prevented depletion of soil through crop rotations or fallow years. Slavery was common in the Middle East, but in Israel it was regulated to protect those who were more like self-indentured servants, including six-year time limits followed by mandatory freedom (Ex. 21:2). Also, some of the extreme penalties were seldom or never invoked, or at least there is limited record of them being enforced. Compare this to America, where treason is the only specific crime named in the Constitution and may be punishable by death—although many historians claim that there has never been a federal execution for treason in U.S. history.[3]

All of this comes back to broad evangelical agreement on the authority of the Bible. There may be discussion or debate over specific issues, but most evangelicals claim the Bible as their final authority. Take capital punishment as an example. Proponents of capital punishment will open their Bibles and find that executions were sanctioned by God. Opponents of capital punishment will open their Bibles and find that two or three eyewitnesses were required, that executions were rare, and that several Bible heroes were unexecuted reformed murderers, including Moses, David, and Paul. Yet both sides of the discussion agree on the authority of the Bible. The Bible is central to evangelical faith and identity.[4]

AGREEMENT ON LIFE

Evangelicals agree that human life comes from God, that all humans are created in God's image, and that human life is to be protected and preserved. This conviction flows out of the Bible's teaching about human creation in Genesis 1:27 and extends through the Old Testament laws defending and fulfilling life from pregnancy to death and in the New Testament promise of eternal life for all who believe in Jesus as Savior and Lord.

Although rooted in the Bible,[5] the evangelical advocacy for life became a political advocacy following the 1973 Supreme Court ruling in *Roe v. Wade* that legalized abortion on demand across the country. Even though the Bible doesn't speak directly to the laws and procedures of abortions as then legalized, evangelicals joined with Catholics in defending the life of the unborn child as a higher moral mandate than the choice of the pregnant woman. Promoting laws, filing briefs with courts, establishing counseling centers, and persuading women and couples have all been tactics shared by evangelicals in the pro-life movement.

Some call the abortion debate a "stalemate" in American law and politics because polls report similar size support for both sides.[6] The nation is divided, as much of the focus has moved from the legalization debate on abortion to the availability debate on abortion with new laws calling for waiting periods and ultrasounds and placing earlier legal limits on abortion procedures. Most polls and news stories report evangelicals as the most consistently pro-life religious group, with the highest pro-life percentages matching the highest church attendance frequency. In other words, the more likely evangelicals (and Catholics) are to attend church services, the more likely they are to be pro-life.

An increasingly vocal element of evangelicals, especially among younger adults, is expanding the pro-life call beyond abortion to child protection, child nutrition, anti-poverty, education, and opposition to capital punishment. These advocates insist that God's gift of human life should be protected and nurtured throughout life and not just until birth. Anti-abortion pro-life groups have pushed back on this as a dilution of the pro-life message, insisting that multiple issues detract from the primary issue of protecting the unborn and muddy the waters with extraneous issues.

Not all evangelicals are pro-life, but most are. Opposition to abortion and putting limits on abortion are more influential in the political choices of evangelicals than any other religious group. Does this mean that evangelicals will vote for a pro-life candidate even if they disagree with many of the candidate's other policies? For many the answer is "yes." For others the answer is "it depends," because they may decide that other priorities are more important in a current election cycle when abortion laws are not likely to change anyway. However, the "it depends" voters should remember that future presidents nominate Supreme Court justices, future senators vote to confirm nominees, and future Supreme Court justices will decide on abortion laws.

AGREEMENT ON RELIGIOUS FREEDOM

Evangelicals agree that religious freedom is every American's right under the Constitution and that erosion of religious freedom is bad for America and bad for evangelicals.

It is an interesting concern, because most Christians in most places through most of history have not had a legal right to religious freedom. Christians have often flourished under restrictions and persecution. Examples range from the Roman Empire to the People's Republic of China to parts of Africa—all places where the church has grown in numbers and influence despite government opposition.

Christians want to worship God and live out their faith without government interference. And evangelical Christians want to evangelize—share their faith with unbelievers with the hope they will become followers of Jesus.

Religious freedom is not just a right to worship in a building with those of similar faith. Religious freedom extends to living out faith at home, raising children, being in the workplace, and having public discourse. This freedom isn't just for Christians; it's for everyone of every faith. Of course, this is not an absolute freedom; no religion should be permitted to conduct human sacrifices or overthrow the government. However, advocates for religious freedom insist that favor should go to the practice of faith, not to the restrictions from government.[7]

The freedom to evangelize is based on the New Testament teachings of Jesus, but is also consistent with the American ideal of allowing all voices to be heard and all persons to be permitted to persuade others to their beliefs. We do this with news stories, commercial advertising, and political partisanship, and we should have equal freedom to persuade others with our religious message.

Religious freedom is called the "first freedom," because it starts the Bill of Rights with the First Amendment to the U.S. Constitution: "Congress shall make no law respecting an establishment of religion, or prohibiting the free exercise thereof; or abridging the freedom of speech, or of the press; or the right of the people peaceably to assemble, and to petition the Government for a redress of grievances."

Many evangelicals fear that religious freedoms will be restricted or curtailed under the premise that freedoms will be used to discriminate against fellow Americans, seek exemptions from government laws with which religious people disagree, and shelter speech that some consider to be hateful. Ironically, restrictions on religious freedom in Europe were the reason many of the first settlers crossed the ocean to establish a new nation where religious freedom would be protected.

There has been and currently is strong support for religious freedom among evangelical Christians, and we may expect that support to grow stronger in future political choices and votes.

AGREEMENT ON MARRIAGE AND FAMILY

Evangelicals agree that God instituted marriage and established families before there were any governments or politics. The Bible describes the family of Adam and Eve and their children and grandchildren predating any nations or civil laws.

This belief is certainly not limited to Christians or those who read the Bible. Marriages and families are universal. Couples and children cross borders, learn new languages, change citizenship, and follow different laws, but they stick together as husband and wife with sons and daughters. When governments divide couples and families through laws, wars, or slavery, there is an instinctive reaction that this is wrong.

Christian weddings are common in American culture with a clergy pronouncement, "As a minister of the gospel of Jesus Christ, I pronounce you husband and wife in the name of the Father, the Son, and the Holy Spirit. Amen."

Churches actively work to strengthen marriages and families with premarital counseling, marriage classes, couples retreats, financial seminars, marriage sermons, divorce recovery workshops, child baptisms and dedications, weekly Sunday schools, youth groups, tutoring, annual vacation Bible schools, children's sermons, church camps, and more. To the inquisitive outsider, many churches could seem to be primarily about marriages, children, and families.

As the United States and several other nations have added a new legal category of marriage, evangelicals have continued to advocate the biblical definition of marriage as a lifetime covenant relationship between one man and one woman. This perspective continues the beliefs and practices of churches for two thousand years and is held by two billion Christians around the world today. Many in America have adopted the new legal category of marriage as compatible with Christian beliefs, but these people are primarily within traditions not usually described as evangelical.

The commitment to the traditional understanding of marriage and family is rooted in biblical teaching and nearly universal church practices throughout history and today. It is not based on animosity toward laws or persons who do not agree with or practice biblical marriage.

WHAT DO THESE AGREEMENTS MEAN?

There are more points of agreement among evangelicals, but these four top most lists. Do they explain how all evangelicals will vote? No, but they do point in some clear directions.

Compare two children who were born in the same hospital on the same day and are growing up in the same neighborhood. One is dreaming about becoming an NFL linebacker and playing in a Super Bowl, and the other is hoping to become a horse jockey who will win a Triple Crown. Before predicting which one is which, be sure to notice that Sam is five feet, two inches tall and weighs eighty-seven pounds, while Sean is six feet, four inches tall and weighs 230 pounds. Since they are both just sixteen years old, we can't be totally sure how tall or heavy they will be when full grown. But it's not too hard to guess which one will most likely head toward the racetrack and which one will head toward the football field. It's still their choice, but the hints are significant.

Christians who agree on the authority of the Bible, the value of life, religious freedom, and marriage and family aren't always predictable in their political choices, but they share convictions in common.

Chapter 8

WHAT TO DO ABOUT POVERTY

"Guuuu...." That's the sound four-year-old Justice makes when imitating the noise that comes out of his stomach at night. It's the parasites inside him. "In the night when we sleep, you can hear them making noises in his belly," according to his mother, Donavine.

Justice lives in Burundi, where he doesn't get enough food to be a healthy child, and the parasites make everything worse because they leech away the nutrients from the food he does eat. At four years old he's the size of a two-year-old. His growth has been stunted.[1]

Parasites can be killed by medicines that aren't all that expensive. But when drugs are in short supply and you are poor, the price in American dollars doesn't much matter.

Poverty isn't really about money. Poverty is about not having food, health, safety, and education—and the hope to go on for another day.

As Christians who love our neighbors, we want to help this boy with parasites even though he lives in the middle of Africa. Do we feel his pain?

EMPATHY?

Our attitudes about poverty and how these attitudes affect our voting depend on how we feel about four-year-olds like Justice. Some of us picture our own young children plagued with parasites, and we cry. Some of us may distance ourselves and say it's somebody else's problem.

Empathy is usually defined as the ability to understand and share the feelings of another. Some researchers insist that we are all hard-wired to be empathic; empathy is part of what makes us human.

It's troubling when other research shows that empathy decreases as statistics about problems increase.[2] For example, empathy soars when hearing about four-year-old Justice, but diminishes when hearing that more than 30,000 children die every day of poverty-related causes. Poverty takes the life of a child every three seconds.[3]

In other words, we care less and do less as we discover the millions who are vulnerable, suffering, and poor. Why is this? Proposed answers vary: (1) Americans are more narcissistic with every generation; we prefer to care about ourselves rather than care about others; (2) We feel we can make a difference helping one person, but are overwhelmed when the numbers far exceed our personal capacity; so we just give up; (3) Some believe in Social Darwinism—that the strong should see their wealth and power increase and the weak should see their wealth and power decrease (that is, the rich get richer and the poor get poorer).

WHO ARE THE POOR?

A wealthy Minnesota businessman decided that his children should see some poor people living in Minneapolis. He drove his family into an urban area to look around and maybe volunteer to help. At the end of their day of exploration he told his children that the people they saw weren't really poor because of the television antennas on the roofs of the houses and apartment buildings where they lived. He explained that truly poor people can't afford TV.

But maybe they really were poor. Those antennas may have been fifty years old and not wired to anything. In a generation with flat-screen, high-definition television connected to cable, the old tube-type sets are available for free—even to poor people. Maybe the residents of those houses and apartment buildings are unemployed and undernourished, lacked medical care, and didn't have heat this winter. Maybe poverty isn't about antennas after all.

Poverty is complicated. Measuring poverty just in dollars ignores health, housing, child mortality, sanitation, inequality, and being treated with dignity and respect. Almost a billion people have no access to clean water, and nearly 2.5 billion don't have adequate sanitation. Lack of water means no irrigation to grow crops. Lack of adequate sanitation leads to diarrhea—500,000 children die each year from diarrhea because of dirty water and poor sanitation (that's over 1,400 per day).[4] Moms and dads love these children and will do anything they can to save their lives, but there isn't much they can do without some outside help.

Because poverty can be different depending on where people live, here are some ways of thinking about it:

- Absolute poverty describes the poorest of the poor who can barely survive in their need for food, clothing, and shelter. It is absolute in that it is the same everywhere—the number of calories required to avoid starvation is constant in every country, culture, and generation. The absolute poor live on $1.25 per day or less—and they number over one billion people. Another 2.2 billion live on less than $2 per day.[5]

- Relative poverty describes the lives of people who are below the minimum living standard of the majority of people in a country. This varies from one country to another, is usually determined by each country's government, and often varies in different parts of the same country.[6]

Most of the world's extremely poor (80%) live in South Asia (399 million) and sub-Saharan Africa (415 million).[7] Combined, these poor populations add up to nearly three times the total population of the United States. So, obviously, our nation has far fewer extremely poor people than most of the rest of the world. But 45.3 million Americans—14.5% of our population—live in relative poverty.[8]

Poverty in America was greatest in the eighteenth and nineteenth centuries, but took a dip with the Industrial Revolution, free and universal high school education, and a rapidly expanding middle class. We became proud of the stories and statistics of millions of Americans who rose out of poverty into better living wages, home ownership, good health care, company pensions, and children going to college for the first time in family history. The dream of our Declaration of Independence became a reality for millions of twentieth-century Americans: "We hold these truths to be self-evident, that all men are created equal, that they are endowed by their Creator with certain unalienable Rights, that among these are Life, Liberty and the pursuit of Happiness."

The dream-come-true of the last century is shrinking with the middle class in this century. Industrial jobs with good wages are fewer, retail and service jobs with lower wages are more common. Long employment with the same company is being replaced with serial employment. Company pensions have diminished, and the Great Recession brought record numbers of home foreclosures. Since 2000, the middle class has been shrinking in all fifty states.[9] What difference does this make? The financial rule of thumb is that no more than 30 percent of family income should go toward housing.[10] In many states families struggle to own a home or rent an apartment because costs have risen and income hasn't. Especially concerning is how much harder it has become for individuals to rise out of a lower class into the middle class. America is much more of a two-class society—its citizens stuck in the lower or remaining in the upper class where they were born and raised.[11]

The statistics can become overwhelming and dull our empathy for the poor. However, for every one of the billions of poor people in our generation, the reality of poverty is personal—all about children, family, and trying to make it in life.

GOOD NEWS/BAD NEWS

The good news about poverty is that enormous progress has been made, especially for the elderly. Early in the twentieth century the poorest Americans were those over sixty-five years old. The majority were women, because women generally live longer than men. As recently as 1980, 23 percent of seniors were poor, but by 2010 the number of elderly poor dropped to 11 percent.

The biggest explanation for this improvement is the start of Social Security in 1935. Back then, only one out of twenty-five Americans were over sixty-five; now, in the twenty-first century, one out of every eight Americans is over sixty-five. And the number is rapidly growing with life expectancy projections few could have imagined a century ago.[12] The news is good because poverty and advanced age are a potent mix when retirees may be too old and too ill to go back to work and provide for themselves.

More good news comes from the spectacular and unprecedented drop in worldwide extreme poverty. In 1990 the countries of the world joined with leading development agencies to adopt the Millennium Development Goals. Goal 1 was to reduce by half the number of people living on less than a dollar per day by 2015.[13] This goal may have seemed unrealistically ambitious to many at the time, but the goal was reached five years ahead of schedule in 2010[14]–with a reduction of nearly one billion people.[15]

Sadly, there is also bad news. While the number of seniors in poverty dropped in America, the number of children in poverty rose from 10 percent in 1980 to 27 percent in 2010.[16] Most of the international decline in poverty was concentrated in China, while India and much of Africa continue to have high infant mortality rates, malnutrition, illiteracy, and unemployment.

Remember: Empathy goes down as statistics go up.

2000+ MEANS IT'S REALLY IMPORTANT

The Bible says more about poverty than it says about heaven, church, marriage, or baptism. The American Bible Society offers a Bible "highlighting more than 2,000 verses that wake us up to issues of poverty and justice."[17] Compassion International, a Christian child sponsorship organization, has a website list citing Bible references to children and poverty.[18] People in poverty must be really important to God to get so much space in the Bible.

Deuteronomy 15:11 is a good place to start as long as we quote the whole verse and don't stop in the middle: "There will always be poor people in the land. Therefore I command you to be open-handed toward your fellow Israelites who are poor and needy in your land." Generosity toward the poor isn't optional. Because there *are* so many poor people in the world, we must act on their behalf.

Use the search box on a computer Bible to look up all the Bible says about the "poor."[19] Check out related terms such as "widow" and "orphan." Here are seven Scriptures as a sample to get started:

- *Deuteronomy 15:7–8, 10:* "If anyone is poor among your fellow Israelites in any of the towns of the land the LORD your God is giving you, do not be hardhearted or tightfisted toward them. Rather, be openhanded and freely lend them whatever they need…. Give generously to them and do so without a grudging heart; then because of this the LORD your God will bless you in all your work and in everything you put your hand to."

- *Psalm 140:12:* "I know that the LORD secures justice for the poor and upholds the cause of the needy."

- *Proverbs 29:7:* "The righteous care about justice for the poor, but the wicked have no such concern."

- *Ezekiel 16:49:* "Now this was the sin of your sister Sodom: She and her daughters were arrogant, overfed and unconcerned; they did not help the poor and needy."

- *Zechariah 7:10:* "Do not oppress the widow or the fatherless, the foreigner or the poor. In your hearts do not think evil of each other."

- *Mark 10:21:* "Jesus looked at him [the rich man] and loved him. 'One thing you lack,' he said. 'Go, sell everything you have and give to the poor, and you will have treasure in heaven. Then come, follow me.'"

- *Luke 14:12–14:* "Jesus said to his host,… 'when you give a banquet, invite the poor, the crippled, the lame, the blind, and you will be blessed. Although they cannot repay you, you will be repaid at the resurrection of the righteous.'"

When Jesus preached in his hometown synagogue, he defined the focus of his life and ministry by quoting from the Old Testament prophet Isaiah: "The Spirit of the Lord is on me, because he has anointed me to proclaim good news to the poor" (Luke 4:18).[20]

Jesus started with those on the margins of society. He often clashed with the rich and powerful, but was pursued and loved by the poor, sick, imprisoned, and oppressed.

If God has a heart for the poor, we should have hearts for the poor. If Jesus prioritized the poor, his followers should prioritize the poor.

The hundreds of Bible references go beyond description to action. They range from individual responsibility to community and government action. Some are general calls to help the poor by giving to them and not oppressing or doing evil to them. Some are specific calls to help the poor, such as Jesus saying, "Go, sell everything you have and give to the poor" (Mark 10:21), and "When you give a banquet, invite the poor" (Luke 14:13).

Beware of those who broadly criticize the poor and blame them for their poverty. Be cautious around those who choose politics that ignore and neglect the poor. None of these are getting their ideas from the Bible. The Bible has strong pro-poor statements from the beginning to the end.

Jesus invites his followers to love and serve the poor the way he loved and served the poor. He even taught eternal accountability for how we treat those in need:

"When the Son of Man comes in his glory, and all the angels with him, he will sit on his glorious throne. All the nations will be gathered before him, and he will separate the people one from another as a shepherd separates the sheep from the goats. He will put the sheep on his right and the goats on his left.

"Then the King will say to those on his right, 'Come, you who are blessed by my Father; take your inheritance, the kingdom prepared for you since the creation of the world. For I was hungry and you gave me something to eat, I was thirsty and you gave me something to drink, I was a stranger and you invited me in, I needed clothes and you clothed me, I was sick and you looked after me, I was in prison and you came to visit me.'

"Then the righteous will answer him, 'Lord, when did we see you hungry and feed you, or thirsty and give you something to drink? When did we see you a stranger and invite you in, or needing clothes and clothe you? When did we see you sick or in prison and go to visit you?'

"The King will reply, 'Truly I tell you, whatever you did for one of the least of these brothers and sisters of mine, you did for me'" (Matt. 25:31–40).

Imagine this preview of all of us gathered before God and getting a report on how we provided food, clothes, medicine, and prison visits to the poor. Jesus gave this dramatic picture to teach the importance of caring for the least of his brothers and sisters.

FAITH THAT WORKS

How do we connect the Bible's teaching about the poor with the reality of more than one billion extremely poor people in the world? What can we do about poverty at home and abroad? The New Testament writer James grappled with this question: "Suppose a brother or a sister is without clothes and daily food. If one of you says to them, 'Go in peace; keep warm and well fed,' but does nothing about their physical needs, what good is it? In the same way, faith by itself, if it is not accompanied by action, is dead" (James 2:15–17). Consider some actions to help the poor:

1. BE PASSIONATE ABOUT BEING COMPASSIONATE.

Ronald Reagan said, "We are a humane and generous people and we accept without reservation our obligation to help the aged, disabled, and those unfortunates who, through no fault of their own, must depend on their fellow men."[21] Conservative political economist Arthur C. Brooks adds that Reagan "recognized the moral truth that a real social safety net is one of the great achievements of our free market system."[22]

Political liberals and conservatives have their proposals about how to help poor people, often inspired by the work biblical Christians are already doing. Christians go to the poorest countries to open clinics, start schools, and help rebuild after wars and disasters. Christians run rescue missions in inner cities and provide foster care in rural towns. We are on the side of poor people. We really care—not because of political parties or policies, but because we are followers of Jesus, believe the Bible, and love the poor.

When it comes to voting for candidates or on initiatives aimed at helping the poor, be well-informed. Study the issues. Ask questions. When politicians promise to help the poor, look for specific examples of what they've done in the past and what they say they will do if elected. Consider whether their proposals include both help with immediate needs and a plan to help people who can work find employment that will permanently lift them out of poverty. Passion based on misinformation can be worse than no passion at all. Compassion that is misdirected can do more harm than good.

2. MAKE A PERSONAL COMMITMENT TO DO ONE THING TO HELP THE POOR, AND FOLLOW THROUGH.

Sign up to sponsor a child through World Vision. Offer to help sponsor a refugee family through World Relief. Volunteer to be a Big Brother or Big Sister or mentor ... and stick with the same child and family for enough years to make a difference. Sign up as a counselor at a nearby Salvation Army office.[23]

What does this personal involvement have to do with how we vote? Knowing individuals, families, and communities in poverty can change our thinking and our voting. We want to be like Jesus, who befriended the vulnerable and needy and spoke out of friendships rather than out of secondhand information.

3. SPEAK UP FOR THE POOR.

Many poor people don't have the means to speak up for themselves and wouldn't be heard if they did. We can sound like Jesus and speak on their behalf. Defend the poor when they are criticized or condemned because of their poverty. Whenever possible, bring them into the conversation so they can speak for themselves. People are less likely to speak disrespectfully of others when actually in their presence. Beware of reading stories about criminals who rip off public assistance programs that lead us to assume that everyone who receives public assistance is lazy and dishonest. Remember that similar stories can be told about rich criminals who cheat on income taxes, but this doesn't mean that all rich people are crooks. Talk about helping the poor at church, in home Bible study groups, at political caucuses, and around the family dinner table. Be a voice for the voiceless.

4. LET POLITICAL CANDIDATES KNOW THAT YOU WANT THEM TO MAKE POVERTY A PRIORITY.

Some good we can do alone; some good we can only do together. The small fire in our kitchen can be extinguished with a personal fire extinguisher; forest fires burning thousands of acres require government agencies and resources. The same goes for helping the poor. We can assist the neighbor down the street, and our church can provide a food shelf. But it takes a team effort to feed millions of undernourished children.

Most candidates for political office are bombarded with questions about taxes, social policies, and current events. Ask what they will do for poor people in the community and nation. Ask at town hall forums, call the candidate's office, write letters, send emails, and recruit friends to do the same. When candidates hear that potential voters care about the poor, they will care about the poor.

5. VOTE TO KEEP THE SAFETY NET STRONG.

When politicians promote policies and budgets that forget about the survival needs of the poor, ask them to make the "safety net" a priority. What is the safety net? It is the web of protection and assistance for people who have fallen into danger through poverty. Churches, charities, and governments step in to provide food for the hungry, housing for the homeless, and medical care for the sick. In the New Testament, Paul took offerings across the Roman Empire and delivered the money to assist the poor in Jerusalem (see Rom. 15:26–28). Today employers pay into worker's compensation insurance to care for employees who are injured on the job. Our state governments help with unemployment compensation for those who lose their jobs in a recession or depression.

Vote for those who want to help feed hungry children, keep families together, make schools strong, provide basic health care, and get the unemployed back to work.

What about helping the poor in other countries? American Christians rejoice when we realize how many millions of poor people have been helped through our country's foreign aid. Then there are some who wonder if we aren't too generous with foreigners when we have our own needs at home. When on-the-street interviewers ask people what percentage of the federal government's annual budget goes to foreign aid, a frequent answer is "25 percent."[24] When asked how much it should be, many say "10 percent" (perhaps reflecting the Christian tradition of tithing—90% for us and 10% for others). The correct answer is around 2 percent, but that includes military aid and loans. The actual foreign aid to feed the hungry, provide clean water, stop children from dying of malaria, halt HIV/AIDS, and other humanitarian assistance is less than 1 percent of our federal budget.

When Americans get the facts and learn that our foreign aid helps save so many lives with just 1 percent, they say it ought to be more. As Christians who believe the teaching of John 3:16 that "God so loved the world," we should insist that humanitarian foreign aid be increased and certainly not decreased.

6. MAKE A LIST OF "POOR PEOPLE I KNOW."

We have all made lists of friends—to invite to a birthday party or to pray about every day. Suppose we made a list of the poor people we know. One name should go at the top of our list of "poor people we know." The top name is "Jesus." Here's how the Bible describes him: "For you know the grace of our Lord Jesus Christ, that though he was rich, yet for your sake he became poor, so that you through his poverty might become rich" (2 Cor. 8:9).

Since Jesus became poor for us, we can advocate for the poor in Jesus' name.

Chapter 9

A NATION OF MINORITIES

Time machines are science-fictional fantasy, but it can be fun to imagine going back to see what America was like in earlier generations. So let's pretend that we could count the population when Columbus landed in 1492. Estimates range from 2.1 million to 18 million.[1] None of them speak English because they are all Native Americans who speak a variety of languages.

Turn the dial on the time machine one century forward to 1592 and meet thousands of immigrants living in Florida and all speaking Spanish because they came from Spain.

Travel north to Virginia and Massachusetts in 1610 and listen to the distinctly English accents of all 350 settlers. Twenty years later, the wave of English immigrants, along with newcomers from Holland, Germany, and other parts of Europe has spiked the northeast immigrant community to 4,646.[2] Keep traveling through the centuries. Listen to the languages of Europeans along the East Coast, Africans primarily in the South and Asians mostly in the West.

Immigrants kept coming—to escape religious persecution in England, potato famine in Ireland, and high unemployment in southern Italy. Immigrants arrive from China to provide inexpensive labor in mines and to build the transcontinental railroad—until Congress stops them in the only race-based immigration prohibition in American history, the Exclusion Act of 1882, because of popular fear of Chinese immigrants in primarily white America.[3]

Some immigrants come for adventure, some to escape poverty, some under the duress of human slavery, and some to reunite families. Many come to follow the American dream in "the land of the free and the home of the brave," described in the words of our national anthem. The biggest flow comes from Europe and brings a variety of customs and languages, but these immigrants are mostly Christian by religion and become fluent in English by the second generation. The numbers grow past 300 million by the twenty-first century as all these immigrants multiplied to develop the most prosperous, democratic, and powerful nation on earth.

They are us.

FROM ONE MAJORITY TO MANY MINORITIES

White immigrants from Europe and their descendants surpassed Native Americans as the majority race of the United States. Our nation has had racial, cultural, and religious diversity since the Pilgrims arrived in Plymouth—but has primarily had a large majority and many minorities. Now this situation is changing.

Since a majority requires 50%-plus, there will be only minorities by 2044 when whites are estimated to make up 49.7% of the population, Hispanics 25%, blacks 12.7%, Asians 3.7%, and multiracial persons 3.7%.[4] This demographic shift to all minorities has already occurred in three states (California, New Mexico, and Texas) and 266 counties, including Broward and Orange counties in Florida, Gwinnett County in Georgia, Prince William County in Virginia, Montgomery County in Maryland, Passaic and Union counties in New Jersey, and Suffolk County in Massachusetts. There are many more, mostly in the South and along the high population areas of the coasts. (Those 266 counties are only 11 percent of the total 2,440 U.S. counties, but they are home to 31 percent of the U.S. population.)[5]

What's happening and what difference will the demographic shift make? There are lots of answers.

- The white population aging and dying faster than babies are being born is the primary reason for this majority demographic shift.[6]
- Birth rates are higher among parents of color.[7]
- Children under age five (in 2014) number more than 20 million, and 50.2 percent of them are minorities.[8]
- The gap in academic achievement between children of different races has decreased, but the gap between rich and poor kids within each racial group is increasing. Class is becoming a more important factor than race in predicting school performance.[9]
- Immigrants over the past fifty years have increasingly come from continents other than Europe.
- Marriages between persons of different races have reached an all-time high and are increasing.[10]

Different parts of America are changing at different rates. Hawaii has never had a white majority. Between 1960 and 2010, Washington, DC, had a black majority. Vermont, Maine, New Hampshire, West Virginia, Iowa, and Wyoming are all more than 90 percent white. Maryland, Mississippi, and Georgia are all trending to be the next "majority minority states" made up of all minority groups rather than a majority of one group.

We don't know all the differences these shifting demographics will make in our nation. Past trends have been toward broader acceptance of diversity, some groups retaining their ethnic identity in the midst of changes around them, and immigrants assimilating for two generations and then recapturing their heritage in the third generation amid ongoing redefinitions of ethnic and racial identities in each generation.

We may project greater integration among America's multiple minorities, or we may expect that minority groups will cluster and be segregated from other minority groups. Perhaps both will happen—many will integrate, and many will segregate. *The New York Times* columnist David Brooks says,

> Let's make some educated guesses about what the New America will look like. It will almost certainly be economically dynamic. Immigration boosts economic dynamism.... There would also be a lot of upward striving. Immigrant groups tend to work harder than native groups. They save more. They start business at higher rates than natives.[11]

THE BOOK OF ALL NATIONS

The Bible is a book of all nations. The human story begins with Adam and Eve as the parents of everyone. We are all members of the human race, and we are all created in the image of God. Some people may emphasize our many differences, but the Bible begins with our universal unity and continuity.

The prominent place goes to Israel in the Old Testament, but there is an ancient catalogue of nations, languages, and races: Egyptians, Hittites, Babylonians, Assyrians, Canaanites, and more. There are surprising stories of intermarriage (Joseph married an Egyptian named Asenath; Moses married an African), business partnerships (King Solomon and Hiram of Tyre building the temple in 1 Kings 5), and political alliances (Daniel and Nehemiah with Nebuchadnezzar of Babylon and Artaxerxes of Persia). The Bible is a book written in Hebrew, Aramaic, and Greek with words from other languages spread through the texts.

But the greatest teaching about God and human diversity comes in the New Testament.

Colossians 1:15–17 explains that the diversity in our world was created by Jesus Christ and is his gift to us. Sin has messed up the creation and abused this beautiful diversity, but the good news of the gospel is that Jesus breaks down the sinful barriers. "There is neither Jew nor Greek, slave nor free, male nor female, for you are all one in Christ Jesus" (Gal. 3:28).

The miraculous coming of the Holy Spirit reported in Acts 2 is marked by Christians around the world every Pentecost Sunday (fifty days after Easter). While unbelievers thought Pentecost was a funny joke, faithful followers of Jesus knew that it celebrated the amazing diversity of the early church:

> When the day of Pentecost came, they were all together in one place. Suddenly a sound like the blowing of a violent wind came from heaven and filled the whole house where they were sitting. They saw what seemed to be tongues of fire that separated and came to rest on each of them. All of them were filled with the Holy Spirit and began to speak in other tongues as the Spirit enabled them.
>
> Now there were staying in Jerusalem God-fearing Jews from every nation under heaven. When they heard this sound, a crowd came together in bewilderment, because each one heard their own language being spoken. Utterly amazed, they asked: "Aren't all these who are speaking Galileans? Then how is it that each of us hears them in our native language? Parthians, Medes and Elamites; residents of Mesopotamia, Judea and Cappadocia, Pontus and Asia, Phrygia and Pamphylia, Egypt

and the parts of Libya near Cyrene; visitors from Rome (both Jews and converts to Judaism); Cretans and Arabs—we hear them declaring the wonders of God in our own tongues!" Amazed and perplexed, they asked one another, "What does this mean?"

Some, however, made fun of them and said, "They have had too much wine" (Acts 2:1–13).

The Romans governed the most diverse empire in the ancient world, and the church of Jesus Christ grew strong and flourished in that diversity. It was an ideal context for fulfilling Jesus' command to "go and make disciples of all nations" (Matt. 28:19). ("Nations" translates the Greek word *ethne* and refers to people groups, not political governments.)

The diversity of the church extended to leadership. Acts 13:1 names the top prophets and teachers of the influential Antioch church as "Barnabas, Simeon (called "the black man"), Lucius (from Cyrene), Manaen (the childhood companion of King Herod Antipas), and Saul" (NLT). Barnabas and Saul (Paul) were Jews from Israel. Manean was the half-brother of King Herod Antipas of Israel. We aren't told where Simeon came from, but that he was black. Lucius was from Cyrene, a major Greek-language city in North Africa in today's Libya.

In case we have missed the Bible message of diversity and unity at the same time, the book of Revelation concludes with John's preview of heaven: "After this I looked, and there before me was a great multitude that no one could count, from every nation, tribe, people and language, standing before the throne and before the Lamb. They were wearing white robes and were holding palm branches in their hands" (Rev. 7:9).

Heaven is for people from everywhere, with every ethnic label and speaking every language—all brought together in righteousness and peace through Jesus. The diversity of mid-twenty-first-century America will be more like the description of heaven's population than ever before. While we don't expect America to become heaven during this century, we still pray, "Thy will be done on earth as it is in heaven."

GETTING READY FOR TOMORROW

Hide-and-seek is a popular children's game. Counselors sometimes advise parents to introduce the game slowly because it scares some young children. After most of the players hide out of sight, the It-player calls out, "Ready or not, here I come!" and starts to search for those who are hidden.

In many parts of the United States all the hidden players of the coming national majority minority are already out in the open. In other places they are not so obvious and still largely hidden. But the message is the same across the country: "Ready or not, here it comes!" The country is changing and needs to prepare for those changes. With values from the Bible, we can be leaders in getting ready.

As Christians who pray for people from every human subgroup to come to personal faith in Jesus, we foresee the exciting potential of America's many minorities becoming Christian. Our individual witness and church outreach should welcome the spiritual opportunities present and future. However, we also want to think about how this diversity influences our political attitudes and actions.

The goal for Christians should be to get our nation ready for what is coming.

PREPARE CHILDREN FOR THE FUTURE.

Most of America's children under age five belong to current minorities. Our nation needs them to grow up to become farmers, teachers, mechanics, pilots, doctors, pastors, politicians, and workers in all occupations.

If we wait until they are adults and discover they aren't adequately prepared, we will have trouble catching them up. It is scary to imagine the cost of shortages in segments of our labor force or future attempts to train specialists who weren't well educated in high school. This means that investments in education are essential sooner rather than later. Advocates for pre-schools, quality teachers, school counselors, extracurricular activities, school computers, technical training, college preparation, and affordable higher education are thinking long-range and not just short-term.

As much as we like equality in everything, we need to make special investments in certain groups of children. Adequate nutrition for children who are undernourished at home, English as a second language classes for children with a different native tongue, community policing and school security for children who are in danger—these are all going to help claim the full potential of our next generation. Today's votes and taxes can shape tomorrow's entire society.

COMBAT RACIAL WRONGS.

Majority prejudice, ignorance, and mistreatment of minorities can be documented in all nations. The United States has had and still has an often sad and shameful history of discrimination, manipulation, immorality, and hatred toward minorities. Those minorities include African Americans, Jews, Native Americans, Japanese Americans, Chinese Americans, and immigrants from Ireland, Sweden, Italy, the Philippines, and Latin America. Racial wrongs against others may show up in any ethnicity, but we all know that most have flowed from the large white majority. Progress has been made, especially since the 1964 Civil Rights Act and the 1965 Voting Rights Act, but there are still many wrongs that need to be addressed.

Most white evangelical Christians say they are not racists and are quick to tell stories of other-race friends they have and equality actions they have taken. This is always good news. The persistent problems may be better described as "racialization" rather than as "racism." Racialization is more systemic[12]—built into the structures and systems of society in policies, budgets, laws, symbols, practices of government, schools, churches, sports, companies, organizations, advertising, media, housing, and culture. Majority whites have benefited from privileges they don't recognize, while minorities face hidden hurdles to success. The point is not only that racism affects individual attitudes and actions, but also that it permeates whole areas of society.

To change our country now and to prepare for the majority minority that is near, we want candidates for office who are informed, understanding, and committed to the biblical values of justice, equality, and love of all our neighbors. Those candidates' commitments should extend to policing, voting, housing, education, employment, courts, and prisons.

SUPPORT MINORITY LEADERSHIP AND REPRESENTATION.

As a diverse democracy with many minorities, it is becoming increasingly important for minorities to take leadership roles in our government and institutions. Even though people have a natural tendency to want leaders like themselves, we all benefit from diverse leadership. Examples include members of school boards and city councils, legislators in both state houses and Congress, judges, and others. Just as important is minority leadership and representation among school teachers, principals, police officers, county clerks, tax agents, prosecutors, prison guards, and other government jobs.

As a nation of minorities, we should expect something close to proportionate minority leadership and representation. This is good for the country as a whole as well as for each of the minorities.

ELECT CANDIDATES COMMITTED TO REPRESENT ALL.

Proportionate minority leadership and representation doesn't happen in one election. Sometimes it either doesn't work or takes a long time. Without giving up on that goal, we can encourage all political candidates to represent everyone. Elected officials have a legal and moral responsibility to provide for and protect all the minorities in their district and not just their donors, friends, supporters, and political constituents. Sometimes the sign of a great leader is when that leader risks the wrath of supporters to be fair to enemies.

What about people whose beliefs are contrary to the Bible and whose behaviors we believe are sinful? What about groups promoting agendas that are racist, discriminatory, hateful, hurtful, and harmful to our nation, to God's creation, and to us? This is an inevitable challenge with no easy answers. As Christians, our first loyalty is to God's law, not any nation's laws. In extreme cases we may be called to take moral stands that are unpopular and bring down consequences on us. In many cases we need to acknowledge that we disagree but recognize that another lifestyle is legal in our democracy even though we cannot approve.

We should support and vote for politicians who will protect our own religious and other civil rights but also remember that protecting the rights of other minorities can be good for them, good for us, and good for America.

BACK TO THE FUTURE

In our imaginary time travel we pretended to travel back to America in 1492, 1592, and 1610. Now let's turn the science-fiction dial and imagine traveling into the middle and end of the twenty-first century. As society and government were different five hundred years ago, they will be different fifty years from now. Enough will be the same for us to feel at home, and enough will be different to make some of us uncomfortable.

When it comes to the shifting demographics of our nation into all minorities, we have seen enough present previews to have an idea of what to expect. Much of what we have seen has been good, but we have also seen clashes of values, violence against innocent people, and injustices that should frighten us all. How we vote and engage all the minorities will shape the future as we fulfill our responsibilities as citizens of heaven and citizens of the United States.

"And we know that in all things God works for the good of those who love him, who have been called according to his purpose" (Rom. 8:28).

Chapter 10

RECONNECTING SEX, MARRIAGE, FAMILY, AND CHILDREN

"The Kissing Song," an old children's ditty, has kids teasing play-mates who were found kissing (or more likely, thinking about kissing) with these words: "First comes love, then comes marriage, then comes baby in the baby carriage." The kids at least had the sequence right. A more contemporary version might be "First comes sex, then comes baby in the baby carriage, then (if funds permit) comes marriage."

Our culture has decoupled sex from marriage, family, and children.

A corollary of the sexual revolution is the no-fault divorce. The marital vows "for better or for worse, for richer, for poorer, in sickness and in health ... until death do us part" have evolved to a commitment to stay together "until we are no longer compatible," and our laws have accommodated the shift. In most states it is no longer necessary to prove that one or both spouses have violated their solemn vows. Children are the big losers when divorce is fast-tracked.

The sexual revolution has disconnected sex from its place within the protective bonds of marriage. This raises an important question: What is marriage? Amid the high-voltage public debate about same-sex marriage, the basic question of what constitutes a marriage has received relatively little attention. With the historic understanding of a male-female union being abandoned, what other parameters remain? Exclusivity? Permanence? Limited to two unrelated persons? Of a certain age? What interest does the state have in regulating these relationships?

With the changes in marriage patterns have come changes in family structure. Demographer Patrick Heuveine estimates that half of all children can now expect to live in a single-parent household before they are age sixteen.[1] Some children shuttle between two households, while blended families attempt to reassemble Humpty Dumpty in new configurations. Among two-parent households, many are cohabiting, while a few are newly married same-sex couples with children by adoption or from previous marriages. Only 57 percent of children live with their biological, married parents.[2] Even when both parents are present, economic pressures and career choices have made the full-time stay-at-home parent a rare luxury, found mainly among the wealthy and the unemployed.[3]

Sex, marriage, and parenting decisions are personal issues influenced mainly by religion, culture, class, and family background. But public policy plays a role in determining which family arrangements are encouraged, rewarded, and supported. In addition to laws on marriage and divorce, taxes (filing status, rates, exemptions, and credits), policies on parental leave, protection for the unborn, child-care support, and educational options and requirements are all matters determined by our elected leaders and sometimes by judges.

BIBLICAL GUIDANCE

The Bible offers clear guidance on marriage, the family, and sexual relationships. The first two chapters of Genesis tell us that God created human beings in his image, that he made us as sexually complementary males and females, and that he designed us to live in families (see Gen. 1:27–28; 2:4–25).[4] God ordained marriage and family before there were any governments or politics. The family is God's first institution and should be our high priority.

One of the Ten Commandments is to "honor your father and your mother" (Ex. 20:12). This is the only commandment that comes with a specific reward: "… so that you may live long in the land the Lord your God is giving you." A harmonious family increases life expectancy.

The same instructions are found in the New Testament commands for children to obey their parents (see Eph. 6:1; Col. 3:20). The New Testament passages also contain a specific warning to fathers not to exasperate, embitter, or discourage their children; "instead, bring them up in the training and instruction of the Lord" (Eph. 6:4; see also Col. 3:21).

Two of the Ten Commandments address our behavior as sexual beings. The seventh warns against adultery, and the tenth against coveting your neighbor's wife (Ex. 20:14, 17). These and many other biblical passages make it abundantly clear that the precious gift of sexuality is reserved for marriage, and that pursuing sexual relations before or outside of marriage can lead to suffering and tragedy. The story of King David and Bathsheba provides a compelling case study on the personal, social, and political impact of sexual sin (2 Sam. 11).[5] Jesus taught that sexual purity is a matter of the heart as well as of outward actions (Matt. 5:27–28).

The family provides one of the most powerful images of the relationship between God and his people. God is repeatedly referred to as a Father who loves and cares for his children. Jesus taught his disciples to pray to God as "Our Father" (Matt. 6:9) and to find their identity in him.

When Jesus was asked about marriage and divorce he quoted from Genesis:

> "Haven't you read," he replied, "that at the beginning the Creator 'made them male and female,' and said, 'For this reason a man will leave his father and mother and be united to his wife, and the two will become one flesh'? So they are no longer two, but one flesh. Therefore what God has joined together, let no one separate" (Matt. 19:4–6).

These two texts, among others, show us that marriage is designed by God to unite a man and a woman in a lifelong, exclusive union that provides for the nurturing of the children with which God blesses the marriage. Of course, some couples are unable to have children, but raising children is the normal expectation for most families. Children are a great blessing, as both of us will attest, and as the Bible repeatedly celebrates.

The family is designed to reflect the loving communion of the triune God: Father, Son, and Holy Spirit. The family draws its inspiration and strength from "the grace of the Lord Jesus Christ, and the love of God, and the fellowship of the Holy Spirit" (2 Cor. 13:14). Marriage is modeled on the relationship between Christ and his church.[6]

Parents retain the primary accountability for their children's nurture and upbringing, yet this responsibility is shared with the wider community. The church is a fellowship of believers in which each member contributes to the growth and maturity of the others. As the apostle Paul wrote in his letter to the Ephesians, "From him [Christ] the whole body, joined and held together by every supporting ligament, grows and builds itself up in love, as each part does its work" (4:16). Paul is a good example of the benefits of formal schooling outside the home, having studied under Gamaliel, one of the great teachers of his day (Acts 22:3).

PUBLIC POLICY RESPONSES

What laws and public policies should Christians support in the areas of sex, marriage, family, and children? How should Christians respond when the laws do not conform to their biblical understanding? What commitments and values should voters look for in the candidates they support for public office? Here are some of the issues.

1. SEX

Sexual relations outside of marriage were once illegal in almost every state. These laws, however, were notoriously difficult to enforce and subject to abuse—even as they were in Jesus' time.[7] Pluralistic societies obviously have problems deciding whose interpretation of sexual ethics to enforce. Even if consensus is achieved, a government that is strong enough to monitor sexual purity would be very likely to abuse its power in other, unacceptable ways. Consider Afghanistan under the Taliban, where girls were prohibited from studying or working outside the home. Women accused of having sex outside of marriage were publicly stoned, and those with exposed ankles could be flogged.[8]

However, there are certain areas where Christians can influence law and public policy by voting for candidates who take clear and principled stands on these issues.

- *Rape and sexual abuse.* Any forced sexual encounters are justly condemned and punished. Violations of children are particularly devastating. Prosecutors face challenges assessing evidence that often revolves around murky issues of consent and conflicting testimony, so that the guilty—and only the guilty—are punished.

- *Pornography.* Hard-core pornography is readily available on the Internet, in convenience stores, and on cable and hotel video services. Obscene material is increasingly broadcast on the public airwaves. Laws against the broadcast and distribution of pornography have frequently not been an enforcement priority for many attorneys general, police, and prosecutors. Yet the harm caused by pornography is great. Its use is psychologically and spiritually harmful to both users and producers. It can also be addictive.[9]

  Candidates who seek positions in law enforcement and justice should be clear about their commitment to enforcing obscenity and pornography laws, particularly those involving children, and bringing perpetrators to justice. Groups such as the National Center on Sexual Exploitation can provide useful information on how to fight pornography.[10]

- *Contraception.* While Catholics and some other Christians oppose artificial contraception in principle, most evangelicals accept the use of contraceptives within marriage.[11] The federal government allocates substantial funding to programs that provide contraceptives to low-income Americans. Some Christians oppose the allocation of these funds to groups, such as Planned Parenthood, that also perform abortions. Some Christians also oppose federal mandates to include contraception, particularly kinds that can function by aborting a fertilized egg, in employer-provided health insurance plans, when the employer has religious objections to some or all contraception.

The Supreme Court ruled in the *Hobby Lobby* case that religious business owners have the right to protection of their religious beliefs when the government cannot demonstrate that its requirements fulfill a compelling government interest using the least restrictive means.[12]

■ *Protecting pregnant women and their unborn children.*
An abortion ends an unwanted pregnancy that arises, in most cases, from out-of-marriage sexual activity. Abortion has been legal throughout the United States under the Supreme Court's 1973 *Roe v. Wade* decision. But subsequent decisions have clarified that restrictions and limitations on the practice of abortion are allowable.

Advances in ultrasound technology have for many expectant parents personalized the baby in the womb, which has helped lead to a significant drop in the number of abortions performed in the United States. But the number still exceeds one million per year. Pro-life advocates have particularly focused on ending abortions after twenty weeks, when the baby is potentially viable outside the womb and can begin to feel pain. Greater emphasis should also be placed on supporting and protecting vulnerable mothers both during pregnancy and after.[13]

2. MARRIAGE AND FAMILY

Marriage laws differ from state to state. Age and parental consent requirements vary, as do the grounds and waiting periods for divorce, and child custody laws. Since the *Obergefell v. Hodges* Supreme Court decision in 2015, one aspect of marriage law that has been uniform across states is the availability of marriage licenses to any two qualified applicants regardless of gender.[14] Short of a constitutional amendment or a Supreme Court reversal in a future ruling, voters will be unable to change this decision.

What voters can do is support candidates and elected officials who will prioritize strengthening traditional marriages, and who will protect individuals and institutions that maintain a biblical understanding of marriage.

- *Protect freedom for all Americans, and their organizations, to maintain their beliefs about marriage.* Until recently, most Americans supported laws upholding traditional beliefs about marriage. Those who maintain their beliefs about marriage should be respected, not punished. Religious organizations should not be forced to revise their beliefs or practices as the price for maintaining tax exemption, accreditation, licensing, and eligibility to compete for federal grants.

- *Remove marriage penalties in tax and benefit programs.* Programs that target assistance to single parents often have the unintended consequence of making marriage more expensive. Getting married would provide much-needed stability to a family, but it sometimes also means paying more taxes and becoming disqualified from much-needed help. Policies need to make marriage more attractive, not more expensive.

- *Reform easy divorce laws.* President Ronald Reagan, himself divorced, once said that his greatest regret as governor of California was signing the state's no-fault divorce law.[15] Allowing a husband or wife to challenge a divorce filing, especially when children are involved, has been shown to reduce the divorce rate. Longer waiting periods also prevent impulsive divorces.

- *Reduce stress faced by low-income families.* Marriage is hard work! When you add the constant struggle to make ends meet, it can become overwhelming. Measures that help working families escape poverty also have the effect of strengthening marriages. For that reason they are doubly important.

3. CHILD CARE AND PRESCHOOL

Children are a blessing from God, but they can be an expensive blessing. Babies follow their own schedules and need constant supervision. The best care children can get usually comes from their own parents.[16] Starting in the womb and during the critical early years, a child's brain develops rapidly. Babies need to connect with caring adults who respond to their attempts to communicate. This interaction, says sociologist Robert Putnam, most typically comes from the child's parents.[17]

But can a family afford to live on only one full-time income, or two part-time incomes, so that one parent is always at home? For some, the answer lies in simple living, an intentional choice to forego optional expenses in order to prioritize being available to their children. For others, this is not a realistic option, and certainly it is not possible for most single parents. Here are some policies that could help parents of young children, and that evangelicals should expect their candidates to support.

- *Provide family and medical leave insurance.* The birth of a child is an exciting, overwhelming time in any family. Parents, both mothers and fathers, need time off from work to care for the new addition to the family. Some employers provide paid or unpaid parental leave for varying periods. But there are no standard benefits guaranteed to all parents. Many parents cannot afford to take unpaid leave from their jobs. In most wealthy countries, paid leave is provided, often funded through employment insurance systems. Critics raise concerns about the impact on small employers. But an insurance plan would allow benefits to be paid through the insurance fund rather than the directly affected employer. The burden would thus be fairly shared by all employers and workers and would not lead to discrimination by employers seeking to avoid hiring prospective parents.

- *Empower parents.* Government funding and tax credits for child care should be available to families who do their own child care, as well as those who pay others for child care. A generous child tax credit available to all parents, or at least to all low-income parents, is preferable to a credit that gives parents incentive not to care for their own children.[18]

- *Use vouchers.* If government funding is made available to support child-care centers in certain areas, it should be provided via vouchers to eligible parents, who may then choose the provider that best meets their children's needs. Direct funding of child-care centers brings government regulation and control, complicating the participation of faith-based providers. Voucher funding permits support to religious as well as secular programs, since parents, not the government, are making the choice. Vouchers also create healthy competition and accountability among service providers who must satisfy their customers to stay in business.

- *Promote early childhood education.* New evidence suggests that healthy adult interaction is essential to optimize brain development in young children.[19] Parents play the critical role here, but quality preschool programs may also contribute.

4. K–12 EDUCATION

Education is a major part of raising children. Free, universal public education has long been an American tradition that some consider one of the major reasons for the success of the country.[20] Today our nation has both wonderful schools and inadequate schools. Unfortunately, the students from disadvantaged backgrounds who most need the best schools rarely have access to them. Our schools may no longer be explicitly divided by race, but segregation along socioeconomic lines is still the reality in too many school districts.

Americans spend more than most countries on public education, but our results are not what they could be. Many education specialists recommend having clearer standards and stricter accountability for both teachers and school administrators. One set of standards, called the Common Core, has generated uncommon controversy. Critics say the Common Core federalizes education, while advocates point out that the standards don't specify any particular curriculum or teaching methods, just the outcomes that every student should be expected to achieve.

Choices in the voting booth help determine who serves on the school board and how much of our taxes go to fund local schools. This is one of the closest-to-home engagements in politics available to Christians. Church engagement in local education can transform schools and lives. From tutoring to prayer to sponsoring a local school, Christians can make a difference in the future of our children that goes far beyond marking ballots.

Here are some key issues to consider when evaluating a candidate's education plans:

- *Education equity.* Children should have an equal opportunity to get a great education regardless of the zip code in which they live. School systems should provide incentives for the best teachers and principals to serve in low-income communities.

- *School choice.* Parents should be able to choose between a range of schools, with the funding following the student. School choice, charter schools, tuition scholarship tax credits, and tuition vouchers are some means to achieve this goal. Care must be taken to provide parents with accurate metrics for evaluating the educational options for their children, and to ensure that children in all communities have access to quality schools and a great education.

PUTTING IT ALL TOGETHER

Strong marriages make a nation strong. Healthy families contribute to physical and mental well-being, peaceful communities, stronger economies, and a long list of benefits. When marriages fail, families are dysfunctional, homes are weak, and we all suffer.

Government cannot make marriages succeed and families happy, but it can establish laws and resources that contribute to healthy families and support strong marriages. Investment in marriage and reducing divorce is a shared opportunity for individuals, families, churches, and government.

It is increasingly difficult to find candidates with biblically informed and consistently applied views on sex, marriage, family, and children whose personal conduct lines up with those ideals. Some candidates may articulate attractive values and model upright living, but may not offer public policies that actually support those values. It is important to test rhetoric against the candidate's track record, if there is one, along with the policies that he or she proposes.

What should we do if none of the candidates articulates consistent pro-life, pro-family, or pro-children positions on issues that we care about? In the short term, we may have to choose the lesser-of-two-evils option—but we don't have to stop there. We should challenge both candidates and fellow voters to rethink their positions and also challenge their parties' blind spots. This can create new political space for candidates in both parties to articulate an agenda that Christians can more readily support.

Upholding the sanctity of life and marriage and the priority of caring for children and families is not easy, but it is the task to which we are called as Christians. By our example, as well as by our political engagement, we can work to create a more satisfactory vision for our nation in these areas.

Chapter 11

WHAT WOULD THE STATUE OF LIBERTY SAY TODAY?

The Statue of Liberty may be the most famous and recognizable symbol of the United States around the world. Over four million tourists visit every year.[1] Her likeness has been minted into our coins and printed on our stamps. The ten-dollar bill shows her torch and "We The People" in red ink. Generations of immigrants have crowded the decks of ships, waiting to see her as they sailed into New York harbor. Since its dedication by President Grover Cleveland on October 28, 1886, the Statue of Liberty has been an icon of American immigration.

The journey from proposal to finished product was not easy for this symbol of America. The French designer Frédéric Auguste Bartholdi originated the idea for the statue shortly after the American Civil War, but couldn't get construction started until the 1870s because of political problems in France. He proposed that the statue be a gift from his country to the United States; the French agreed to pay for the statue if America would donate the land and pay for the pedestal. Conservative monarchists in France opposed funding the statue because they said it was a liberal idea. Private fundraising in the United States initially failed, so the New York state legislature offered $50,000 in government money. But this was vetoed by then-Governor Grover Cleveland. Congress declined in 1885 to contribute $100,000 in federal funds.

When writer Emma Lazarus was asked to write a poem, she refused because "she couldn't write a poem about a statue"[2]— although she finally agreed. Her poem was posted on a bronze plaque in the pedestal of the statue in 1903 with words that became an American credo:

> Give me your tired, your poor,
> Your huddled masses yearning to breathe free,
> The wretched refuse of your teeming shore.
> Send these, the homeless, tempest-tossed, to me:
> I lift my lamp beside the golden door.

The process from proposal to completion was punctuated with controversy, delays, financial difficulty, and political arguments. Now, more than a century later, all those problems seem almost silly as we honor the Statue of Liberty as a symbol of what America is all about. In so many ways, its story is similar to the stories of immigrants to America and the U.S. immigration policies—a long and often controversial journey.

Suppose Emma Lazarus were writing her poem today. Would the words assigned to the Statue of Liberty still apply, or would the message have changed?

A WORLD OF REFUGEES AND IMMIGRANTS

Over the past fifty years there have been an estimated 191 million immigrants worldwide.[3] This means that about 3 percent of the world's population has moved from their native countries to other countries. Immigration is concentrated in twenty-eight countries, with Europe having received 30 percent and the United States having received 28 percent.

Scholars explain that immigration has two primary components:

push and pull. Some people are pushed out of their countries by politics, economics, and other pressures. Some people are pulled to new countries by the attractions of freedom, jobs, family, and better lives.

All of this is to say that there is a lot of immigration going on around the world. There always has been. The Bible is full of immigration stories like those of Abraham, Moses, Daniel, the nation of Israel, and Jesus and his family. The United States is largely a nation of immigrants from Europe, Asia, Africa, and the Americas, yet our country has a mixed history when it comes to immigration laws.

CHANGING U.S. IMMIGRATION LAWS

The first European immigrants arrived uninvited by the Native American population. Europeans have received preference in coming to America for most of our history (including today, when visas are not required of tourists). Africans were forced to migrate through slavery. The Chinese were welcomed for cheap West Coast labor and then severely restricted. Japanese immigrants became U.S. citizens and then were located to internment camps during World War II. In recent years, immigrants to the United States from Cuba have been welcomed with benefits because Cuba has been considered our enemy, while immigrants from Haiti have been forced to return because Haiti is considered our friend.

Sometimes there have been very good reasons for American immigration laws, and sometimes they have seemed like nonsense. What we know for sure is that the laws have frequently changed, and it is time to update them once again.

A BROKEN SYSTEM

Even though there may be significant disagreement about what should be changed in our immigration system, just about everyone agrees it's not working very well. Some say the country simply needs to enforce laws already on the books; others say we need new and tougher laws; many say it's time for a comprehensive overhaul. Even though there is broad popular and political agreement that change is needed, there has been an ongoing stalemate that, in essence, ratifies our current broken system.[4]

Immigration issues include hurdles getting visas, access to government agencies, long waiting periods of many years, trying to reunite families of parents and children, a shortage of farm laborers, and limits on getting and keeping high-skilled workers needed in America who can't get visas. Much of the attention has gone to the estimated 11.5 million people who have illegally entered or stayed in the United States and are now "undocumented" immigrants. Their number totals about 3.7% of the country's population, and the majority of them (59%) are from Mexico. Of the 11.5 million, 25% live in California, with other concentrations in Texas (16%), Florida (6%), Illinois (5%), New York (5%), and New Jersey (4%).

We might assume that all who are undocumented crossed our borders illegally, but a surprising number entered with legal visas and simply stayed. According to the Pew Hispanic Center, nearly half of the unauthorized immigrants currently living in the United States entered legally and were subject to inspection by immigration officials. They are called "overstayers."[5] Greater border security is only part of the answer to controlling illegal immigration.

Here's what life is like for many of those 11.5 million undocumented immigrants:

- If an undocumented laborer works hard and does a good job but is underpaid or unpaid, there is little he can do, because he risks deportation if he goes to the authorities.

- If an undocumented woman is raped, she cannot call the police, because she may be forced to leave the country, and that might mean leaving behind her children who were born here.

- If the parents of a child born in America are deported, that child may be forced into foster care or become homeless without parents. He or she cannot legally go with parents who are from Mexico, Central America, or China, because the child is an American citizen without legal status in those places.

- If a teenage boy is suspected of being undocumented, he may be arrested and placed into a detention center, where there is a risk he will be subjected to prison rape while he awaits verification. He may be verified to be a citizen of the United States, but sexually attacked before being released.

- Many children illegally entered the country because of their parents, not through any choice of their own. They speak only English. They have attended American schools and done well. They love this country. Some don't even know that they are not citizens until they apply for college or a job and then are told to leave the country and go to a place where they do not speak the language or know any people.

- Some states have suggested that local police seek out undocumented immigrants and turn them over to federal agents for processing and deportation. Police officers have said that this risks a severe tension between police and many immigrant communities who already are unsure if they can trust the police. If the police can't build relationships and trust with immigrant communities, the job of fighting crime becomes that much harder.

- Some immigrants have waited years for their paperwork to be processed so they can be reunited with their families. They have done everything in full compliance with U.S. laws, but it may take a long time—in some unusual cases up to twenty-five years.

- Millions of workers have jobs, homes, families, and stability, but are using false Social Security numbers. They pay 15.3 percent of their income into the federal Social Security system, but will not be able to collect disability or retirement or Medicare benefits in the future. They pay billions in taxes that benefit others.

We are a country of immigrants that still benefits from immigrants. We are an aging nation with a relatively low birthrate; younger immigrants provide labor, but also pay taxes to support older Americans. Yet, we also have American industries unable to fill many high-skill positions with American citizens. To grow their businesses, they want to hire immigrants, but face laws restricting their access to employees needing visas. There are hundreds of thousands of openings in STEM (science, technology, engineering, mathematics) fields, but only 65,000 visas are granted each year.[6] The quota is filled within weeks and all other applicants are turned away after that.

It is not unusual for immigrant students to earn doctorates in our schools and receive job offers in the United States, yet be forced to return to their homelands because they can't get visas. Business entrepreneurs move their companies overseas so that they can hire the employees they need but can't find here. Farmers have reduced their planted acreage when they can't hire enough immigrants to bring in the harvest. The list goes on in medicine, computer science, and other fields for which our nation is not producing enough skilled workers or our universities are educating them and losing them to competing countries.

Are all immigrant stories and statistics good? They are not. Some immigrants have entered this nation without permission and have committed crimes, organized gangs, sold drugs, and taken unfair advantage of our schools, medical facilities, and social services. Their misbehavior may mimic the crimes of our native-born, but they hurt us all, including citizens and immigrants alike. However, it is neither fair nor true to blame all immigrants for the sins of some.

Our immigration system is broken and needs to be fixed.

NO EASY ANSWERS

How did we get into this situation? There is no single answer. Some say that for many years the United States has given the impression of huge "Help Wanted" signs at our borders followed by "No Trespassing" signs inside the country. It's confusing!

We have had laws that unrealistically restrict immigration, but have often failed to enforce them, have not funded government agencies to operate adequately, and yet have benefitted from the economic growth made possible through immigration.[7]

The political polarization and rhetoric has made a difficult situation worse.

Simple solutions aren't so simple when we get down to details. For example, suppose 11.5 million undocumented immigrants were to be rounded up and deported. Current estimates are that this would take twenty years and cost the government between $400 and $600 billion. Every American would pay an extra $2,000 in taxes to foot the bill. The tougher questions are what to do with the millions of children who are U.S. citizens and left behind, who will take care of those with disabilities and special needs, and do we want to deport elderly undocumented immigrants from nursing care?

On the other end of the debate is the question of how and when illegal immigration can be reduced. It seems impossible to block everyone trying to enter as long as we have a 1,954-mile border with Mexico, a 5,522-mile border with Canada (including the border with Alaska), and 95,471 miles of shoreline. That's 102,947 miles of places to get into the United States, not counting all of our airports.

But we should be able to pass laws and take actions to remove the unnecessary barriers to legal immigration and reduce the flow of illegal immigration. And what about those undocumented immigrants already here? Efforts to keep them are branded as "amnesty," although the definition of *amnesty* is "an official pardon of all who have been convicted of political offenses." Few favor blanket amnesty and instead advocate for penalties short of deportation.

At some point we must move beyond looking back in time for causes and move ahead toward solutions. As Christians, we once again begin with the Bible.

BEGINNING WITH GOD'S WORD

Lifeway Research polled evangelical Christians to find out what most shapes their thinking about immigrants and immigration. The results showed that more than twice as many are shaped by cable news programs than by our Bibles and our churches combined.[8] So the first thing we can do is ask God to teach us from his Book before we turn on our TVs.

For example, the Old Testament offers only three commands to love. It does not command us to love our parents, children, spouses, or nation—all good to love, but we are not commanded to love any of them. Rather, the Old Testament commands us to love God, neighbors, and immigrants:

- *Deuteronomy 6:5:* "Love the LORD your God with all your heart and with all your soul and with all your strength."

- *Leviticus 19:18:* "Love your neighbor as yourself. I am the LORD."

- *Deuteronomy 10:19:* "And you are to love those who are foreigners, for you yourselves were foreigners in Egypt."[9]

With ninety-two Old Testament references to immigrants,[10] we can easily conclude that they matter to God. If you desire to know the mind and heart of God when it comes to immigrants, read those verses.[11] These verses have already influenced many in our evangelical churches; instead of starting with modern laws or current politics, they have started with the Word of God and had their hearts and attitudes shaped by the Bible. Here are seven examples:

- *Leviticus 19:9–10:* "When you reap the harvest of your land, do not reap to the very edges of your field or gather the gleanings of your harvest. Do not go over your vineyard a second time or pick up the grapes that have fallen. Leave them for the poor and the foreigner. I am the LORD your God."

- *Leviticus 19:33–34:* "When a foreigner resides among you in your land, do not mistreat them. The foreigner residing among you must be treated as your native-born. Love them as yourself, for you were foreigners in Egypt. I am the LORD your God."

- *Leviticus 24:22:* "You are to have the same law for the foreigner and the native-born. I am the Lord your God."

- *Deuteronomy 1:16:* "And I charged your judges at that time, 'Hear the disputes between your people and judge fairly, whether the case is between two Israelites or between one of them and a foreigner residing among you.'"

- *Deuteronomy 24:14–15:* "Do not take advantage of a hired worker who is poor and needy, whether that worker is a fellow Israelite or a foreigner residing in one of your towns. Pay them their wages each day before sunset, because they are poor and are counting on it. Otherwise they may cry to the Lord against you, and you will be guilty of sin."

- *Deuteronomy 24:19:* "When you are harvesting in your field and you overlook a sheaf, do not go back to get it. Leave it for the foreigner, the fatherless and the widow, so that the Lord your God may bless you in all the work of your hands."

- *Deuteronomy 26:12:* "When you have finished setting aside a tenth of all your produce in the third year, the year of the tithe, you shall give it to the Levite, the foreigner, the fatherless and the widow, so that they may eat in your towns and be satisfied."

The Bible provides plenty of stories and instructions about immigrants and how they are treated and should be treated. Daniel and Esther are Bible books named after immigrants in foreign lands. Jesus and his family were immigrants to Egypt. Jesus spoke kindly about the good Samaritan when many of his fellow countrymen hated the Samaritans. Throughout the New Testament Christians are called foreigners and strangers in this world. Hebrews 13:2 teaches, "Do not forget to show hospitality to strangers, for by so doing some people have shown hospitality to angels without knowing it."

The overarching message of the Bible on this topic is that immigrants are vulnerable and deserve our special care and attention. While it does not give us details for modern American immigration policies and laws, it orders our values and calls for compassion. As we shape our political thinking and choose candidates, let the Bible help us sort through what we hear on a favorite cable channel or read online.

MANY OF THEM ARE US

Who are these immigrants anyway? You might be surprised to learn that a significant number of immigrants are evangelical Christians who belong to our local churches. One of the fastest-growing evangelical denominations estimates that 40 percent of the denomination's congregations are immigrant and minority churches, and perhaps half of them are pastored by undocumented immigrants.

Many immigrants have either brought their Christian faith with them to America or have become Christians after arriving here. They are clearly the growing edge of evangelicalism in America. For generations American churches have sent missionaries to other countries, and now those other countries are sending missionaries to us.

Perhaps a hundred years from now church historians will explain how immigrants blessed and renewed American Christianity when it might have otherwise atrophied and declined.

AREN'T CHRISTIANS SUPPOSED TO OBEY THE LAW?

Think about Romans 13:1: "Let everyone be subject to the governing authorities, for there is no authority except that which God has established." If we tolerate illegal entry into this country, aren't we supporting lawbreaking, and isn't that contrary to the Bible? Can these undocumented immigrants in our churches be true Christians if they are lawbreakers?

These are important questions. Certainly, those who have broken the law have a responsibility to admit what they have done and make it right. But we also have a responsibility to help them make it right.

Crossing a border to get a job to feed and care for your family is not lawbreaking on the same level as drug-trafficking, gunrunning, terrorism, or murder. Our American legal system has borrowed from the Bible a tiered legal system requiring lesser punishments for lesser lawbreaking and greater punishments for greater lawbreaking. As we often say, "The punishment should fit the crime."

Many of us who are Christians have broken the speed limit laws, the due date for income tax return laws, and probably a lot of other laws. For some crimes the punishment is a reprimand, for some it is a fine, for some it is community service, for some it is jail, and for some it is life in prison. Perhaps the punishment for illegally crossing the border should be a fine for some and deportation for others.

When Jesus' disciples picked grain on the Sabbath, they were accused by the Pharisees of breaking the law. Jesus defended them in two ways: (1) He cited an Old Testament story in which King David was hungry and broke the law by eating consecrated bread from the temple; (2) he taught the principle of people over certain

WHAT WOULD THE STATUE OF LIBERTY SAY TODAY?

laws ("The Sabbath was made for man, not man for the Sabbath," Mark 2:27). In other words, laws are good, important, and necessary, but don't forget about the real needs of real people.

WHAT SHOULD WE DO?

What should we do, and how should we vote? The National Association of Evangelicals conferred with member denominations, evangelical organizations, churches, and individual Christians to draft an approach to immigration reform that is based on the Bible and addresses our broken immigration system. After a long time and a lot of work, a consensus settled on seven principles:[12]

1. That immigrants be treated with respect and mercy by churches. Exemplary treatment of immigrants by Christians can serve as the moral basis to call for government attitudes and legislation to reflect the same virtues.

2. That the government develop structures and mechanisms that safeguard and monitor the national borders with efficiency and respect for human dignity.

3. That the government establish more functional legal mechanisms for the annual entry of a reasonable number of immigrant workers and families.

4. That the government recognize the central importance of the family in society by reconsidering the number and categories of visas available for family reunification, by dedicating more resources to reducing the backlog of cases in process, and by reevaluating the impact of deportation on families.

5. That the government establish a sound, equitable process toward earned legal status for currently undocumented immigrants who desire to embrace the responsibilities and privileges that accompany citizenship.

6. That the government legislate fair labor and civil laws for all residing within the United States that reflect the best of this country's heritage.

7. That immigration enforcement be conducted in ways that recognize the importance of due process of law, the sanctity of the human person, and the incomparable value of family.

We believe that these seven principles can direct us to candidates, policies, and legislation that will align with our biblical faith and be good for our nation. Whether in immediate congressional changes to federal immigration laws or ongoing changes in the future, these principles can provide a template for evaluating political proposals.

What can Christians do?

- Learn what the Bible says about immigrants and how to treat them.

- Research who are the immigrants in your town and congressional district.

- Get to know some immigrants personally. Don't ask them if they are documented or not; get to know them as persons; listen to their stories.

- Look up online the policies, past actions, and future promises of political candidates to see how they align with what the Bible says.

- Communicate with present representatives and competing candidates that immigration is important to you and you want to vote for someone who will take positive biblical actions.
- Promote and vote for candidates who will be God's agents in loving immigrants and fixing our broken system.

ALL AT ONCE OR ONE STEP AT A TIME?

When our politicians address immigration, they often select one or two hot-button solutions rather than the more difficult effort to provide a comprehensive solution. For example, one candidate might call for beefed-up border patrol. Another might promise to fix our immigration problem by creating a legal path to citizenship. As Christians, we must expect more from our candidates. I (Leith) addressed this in a *New York Times* editorial and offer it here to explain why we should make changes all together:

Just about everyone agrees that our national immigration system is broken and needs to be fixed. After years of delay and disagreement, the mood is moving to "sooner" rather than "later."

Unfortunately, one of the points of disagreement is over the label "comprehensive" when it comes to immigration reform.

If your car is out of gas and has a dead battery and a flat tire, it won't help to solve one problem. You need a comprehensive approach.

Let's take the word out of policy and politics and into a discussion with your mechanic.

The two of you are standing in his shop next to your broken car. It's obvious that it won't run and the mechanic explains why: out of gas; dead battery; flat tire; lost key. You are concerned about the cost but really need the car to get to work every day. "If I fixed only one or two of the items on the list, which would you recommend?" The mechanic replies: "If you fix just two, your car will still be broken. For it to run right, you need to fix them all." "Well," you suggest, "suppose we start with a gallon of gas. That's the cheapest and easiest. We'll deal with the others next year."

Finally you make a bold decision and tell him to fix them all at the same time. The goal is not to make your car perfect but to get the car running so you can go to work every morning. It's the right thing to do.

Because the parts of immigration policy are so connected, we need to try our best to fix them comprehensively. Treat everyone with respect. Secure our borders. Authorize guest workers. Keep families together. Provide a path to legal status or citizenship for those in the U.S. illegally. The goal is not perfection but to fix what is wrong and get the systems running. It's the right thing to do.[13]

Chapter 12

WHO PAYS THE BILLS?

Imagine you are at a restaurant having dinner with friends. The food and conversation are great. Some order an appetizer, follow it with steak and lobster, and finish with cheesecake for dessert. Others pick the cheapest thing on the menu.

When the waiter brings the check, most reach for their wallets and put some bills on the table. Some are generous and put in more than enough. One covers for a friend who is unemployed. A few pull out their calculators to figure out exactly how much they owe. And one or two seem to have forgotten to bring any money with them. In the end, the bill is paid, with some paying more than their share and others eating for free. Among friends, this is rarely a problem.

Legislators face the issue of fairness when they try to figure out how to divide up the cost of running the government. Their task is not so easy. No one enjoys paying taxes. Sometimes candidates run on a platform of cutting, or at least not increasing, taxes. But when they get into office, they find those promises hard to keep.

Some public services can be financed by user fees, such as toll roads or issuing a driver's license. If you don't use the service, you don't pay. But it is not practical to charge for most services in this way, because many government functions serve the people as a whole rather than specific users. For example, the ambassador to Japan represents our nation's interests in that country; all of us benefit if we have peaceful relations with Japan and its people. Similarly, the Food and Drug Administration approves the safety and efficacy of medicines before they can be sold in our local pharmacy. Both are funded by our taxes, and rightly so.

There are legitimate debates about what government services we need, as well as who should pay for them. Many voters support cutting the size of government. But they tend to be more supportive of specific government programs and benefits, especially ones that benefit them. Similarly, voters often support lowering taxes on themselves, but are okay with raising taxes on others. A notable exception is that a majority of wealthy Americans believe they pay less than their fair share of the tax burden.[1]

Since both cutting services and asking people to pay taxes are unpopular, legislators are frequently tempted to run up debt—in effect, forwarding the bill to future voters, who may not even be born yet. It would be like the friends at the restaurant asking the waiter to give the check to next year's customers.

It may be appropriate for government to borrow money to finance infrastructure projects, where future beneficiaries pay their fair share of the cost of a road or bridge. And many economists recommend increased spending during economic downturns to revitalize the economy. But much of the current federal deficit has gone to pay for current operating expenses. States and cities also have large debts, including promises they have made to pay for medical and pension benefits for their retired workers.[2]

Few topics evoke as much contentious debate as taxes. Is there a Christian position in this debate?

TAXES IN THE OLD TESTAMENT

Government is, in principle, a gift from God for our good.[3] Our leaders are God's servants in full-time government ministry (see Rom. 13:4–6). Just as ministers in the church deserve to be supported (see 1 Tim. 5:17–18), so do those in public service. When we pay taxes, we fulfill our obligation as Christians as well as our obligation as citizens. We contribute to the common good and help create the conditions in which our communities and our neighbors can flourish.

Of course, not every government initiative blesses the nation or deserves our support. Governments, like the humans who run them, are corrupted by sin. So we should have realistic expectations and build in appropriate safeguards. As citizens in a democracy, we can work to improve our government. We can pray for our leaders, as the Bible commands (1 Tim. 2:1–2). They certainly need God's wisdom.

In a perfect world, we wouldn't need taxes. Citizens would voluntarily contribute to fund the government. Actually, this idea is already being tried. The U.S. Treasury Department's Bureau of the Public Debt accepts tax-deductible contributions from citizens who want to help pay down the national debt. Annual contributions have averaged around $4 million. But we don't live in a perfect world—our government spends that much every 38 seconds.[4] The biblical witness to human greed along with our own experience show that if we were to rely solely on voluntary contributions even for the limited purpose of providing help with food, housing, and medical care to our must vulnerable neighbors, many people would suffer and some would die. Christians and churches do a lot to help, and we could do more, but simple math tells us that we can't meet all the needs on our own.

In 2013, there were around 45.3 million Americans living

below the poverty line,[5] and perhaps 350,000 religious congregations, of all backgrounds.[6] If these congregations shared the load equally, each one would have to help 129 people living in poverty. However, the median American church only has 75 active members.[7] And some of them are living in poverty themselves. If the government's food aid programs were canceled, each church would need to contribute $200,000 each year to replace the lost food, or $50,000 just to help the neediest families—while also maintaining their private food banks and soup kitchens.[8] And this does not count the cost of assisting families who need help with housing or medical care.

While charity is crucial, we also need the government to step in and fulfill its responsibility to care for the poor.

At the same time, our understanding of human depravity clearly warns against giving all power and responsibility to government. The various human experiments with totalitarianism—some justified on the basis of their promise to meet human need—show the danger of overly concentrated power, whatever the rationale. We find this concern about the dangers of concentrated power evident in Moses' instructions to the Israelites about the role of a king in their future governance (Deut. 17:14–20). The emphasis is on what the king is not to do: acquire many horses (for military purposes), acquire many wives, or acquire large amounts of silver or gold. In 1 Samuel 8:6–18 we see a similar warning about the insatiable appetite of the king: "He will take the best of your fields and vineyards and olive groves and give them to his attendants. He will take a tenth of your grain and of your vintage and give it to his officials and attendants" (vv. 14–15). The Bible does not condemn the monarchy as a form of government, but it is honest about the costs.

Elsewhere the Old Testament describes a system of taxes that, even before the period of the kings, funded both the civic and religious functions of the nation of Israel. Among these taxes were the following:

- A basic tax of 10 percent is mandated in Leviticus 27:30. This is, according to Numbers 18:21, meant to support the Levites whose duties spanned both religious and governmental functions. While this is called a tithe, it was not an optional offering, but rather functioned more as a tax.

- An additional 10 percent levy was to be used to cover the costs of participation in the various national feast days, described in Deuteronomy 14:22–27. This was different than a traditional tax in that the taxpayers themselves administered the funds in the course of fulfilling their religious duties.

- A third 10 percent tax was payable only every three years, so essentially it represented a 3.33 percent annual tax. This is described in Deuteronomy 14:28–29 and was designated to care for the needs of the poor.

- An additional rule required farmers to leave part of their crops for the poor to glean—a government welfare system that encouraged work.

When Israel was at various times dominated by Assyria, Babylon, Egypt, or Persia, they were taxed to support those empires.[9] When they could, they in turn used their power to exact tribute from the nations around them.[10] These practices are described, though not necessarily endorsed.

TAXES IN THE NEW TESTAMENT

Jesus discussed taxes in two well-known passages. In Matthew 17:24–27, Peter was asked if Jesus paid the annual temple tax owed by Jewish adult males to support the temple sacrifices.[11] Jesus agreed to pay the tax, which he did for both himself and Peter, by sending Peter to catch a fish that had a coin in its mouth that was exactly the amount of the tax for two. His point was to show that God is a Father who provides for his children, not a human king who depends on his subjects for support.[12] Notably, while Jesus may have disagreed with the tax, he still paid it.

Matthew later on records what has become Jesus' best-known comment on taxes, the instruction to "render to Caesar the things that are Caesar's, and to God the things that are God's" (Matt. 22:21 ESV). When Jesus was charged at his trial with instigating a tax rebellion, it was a false accusation, as Pilate confirmed (Luke 23:2–4).

In upholding Caesar's right to collect taxes, Jesus was not endorsing the Roman emperor. Jesus elsewhere spoke critically about the way the kings of the Gentiles lorded it over their subjects, rather than serving them as Jesus did (Luke 22:25). But Jesus apparently recognized that human governments, in order to function, need revenue. By contrast, God not only doesn't tax his people, but he supports them—even when they have been rebellious.

Beyond the general legitimacy of taxes, there are many questions about who and what should be taxed, and at what levels. The Bible does not tell us whether government should tax wealth, income, trade, or spending, or some combination of these; nor whether all citizens should pay the same amount, the same percentage, or an amount based on what they can afford. That is left for us to figure out, using general biblical principles, reason, and experience.

WHAT TAX POLICIES SHOULD CHRISTIANS SUPPORT?

As you consider various tax proposals offered by candidates, ask yourself if they advance these general principles:

- **Freedom.** All people should have enough income left, after taxation, to have a reasonable opportunity to achieve their God-given potential and fulfill their calling as stewards of God's creation, within a context of peace and security (see Gen. 1:28). This goal is helped by a system of checks and balances that deters governmental abuse of power, and by keeping both taxes and government services at the lowest appropriate level.[13]

- **Fairness.** Those similarly situated should be treated similarly. This does not require that everyone be treated the same. Some argue for flat tax where everyone pays the same percentage. Others point out that the same tax rate could cause considerable suffering for a family that is barely getting by while requiring little sacrifice from a wealthy family. Most could agree that the confiscatory rates of as much as 94 percent, which were in place in the mid-twentieth century, are both unfair and unwise.[14]

- **Family.** Tax policies should encourage marriage and offset some of the costs of raising children with generous child tax credits. Families contribute to the common good by raising the next generation. The tax burden, at least for low-income families, should be reduced accordingly.

- **Human needs.** Citizens, after paying their taxes, should be able to meet their family's basic needs. For low-income workers, this goal can be met by providing tax credits to supplement what they earn through employment as well as through programs of support for basic needs, such as low-income housing vouchers and food aid.

- **Simplicity.** The tax system should be easy to understand, follow, and monitor, to encourage high levels of voluntary compliance and reduce fraud. Providing that a nation's tax system is respected as fair and the government's purposes as legitimate, it should be possible to maintain a tax system with a high level of voluntary compliance.

- **Fiscal responsibility.** The level of taxation should be adequate, over time, to meet current needs, reduce indebtedness, and provide for the future. However, the magnitude of the current debt crisis is such that debt reform will require a disciplined long-term plan. Both sudden increases in taxes or sharp decreases in spending could trigger economic crises that could make the problem worse.

Keep in mind that in a modern economy, taxes play many roles besides raising government revenue. Taxes are also used to encourage desired behavior (for example, savings and investment) and to discourage unhealthy behavior (for example, smoking tobacco or gambling). Both tax and spending decisions are used to regulate the economy, smooth out the ups and downs of the business cycle, and accomplish other public purposes.

PUTTING IT ALL TOGETHER

When we consider what tax proposals to support, we will usually find ourselves juggling competing priorities. We naturally want to pay as little as possible in taxes, but we also want to live in a well-run community, state, and country where citizens are well served and protected.

Learn to look beyond simplistic rhetoric and consider the issues at stake. If something sounds too good to be true, it probably is. If someone says that other people should pay for our government, remember the Golden Rule. And consider this bold act of Christian faith: The next time you pay your taxes, say a prayer for your leaders at every level—school board members, mayor, governor, state legislators, members of Congress, and the president. They are doing God's work and will benefit from your prayers. And the entire nation might as well.

Chapter 13

JUSTICE AND JAILS

Twenty-two-year-old Billy Moore, an Army private with a troubled childhood, returned to rural Georgia in 1974 after a tour of duty in Germany. Arriving home, he found his wife addicted to heroin and living with a drug dealer. Shocked, he took his three-year-old son and moved into a trailer. With bills piling up, he decided to rob an elderly man in his home. When Fredger Stapleton, age 77, tried to defend himself in the dark with a rifle, Moore shot back, killing Stapleton. The next day Moore was arrested and confessed to the murder. At the trial he pled guilty and was sentenced to death.

While in prison, Billy received a visit from a local pastor, who came at his aunt's request. Billy gave his life to Christ and was baptized a week before he thought he was to be executed. In prison he studied the Bible and wrote to Stapleton's family, asking their forgiveness. Stapleton's family forgave Billy and began to advocate for his sentence to be commuted to life in prison. Having lost one family member, they said, they didn't want to lose another.

Billy lived through thirteen execution dates while his appeals were considered, at one point coming within seven hours of being executed. Amazingly, in 1991 Billy was granted clemency and released from prison. He may be the only guilty man ever to be released from an American death row. He has since been ordained and now works in full-time Christian ministry.[1]

Billy's story illustrates both the depths of human depravity and the power of love, forgiveness, and redemption. It also raises questions. How did a man who had served honorably in the military become a thief and murderer? What was the role of generational sin (Billy's father spent seventeen years in prison)? How can violent crime be prevented? How should armed robbers and murderers be punished? Why does our justice system do such a poor job of rehabilitating offenders and restoring victims? And for Christians, how should we vote when issues of crime and punishment appear on the ballot?

FROM EDEN TO SING SING

Try this thought experiment: Suppose that Adam and Eve did not eat the forbidden fruit, and human society developed as God intended, without sin. What kind of legal system would emerge? Presumably there would be no need for prisons or jails. But what about a legislature? Would Eden need one? What about courts? Would there be a need for lawyers and judges to help interpret and apply the laws? As Eden modernized, would its roads need traffic lights? Would the suburbs of Eden require zoning restrictions, to keep homes and factories separate?

If laws and structure are necessary for the smooth functioning of a virtuous society, how much more critical are they in our fallen world. We may complain about our legal system and its shortcomings, but few of us could imagine life in a world without laws. We catch a glimpse of the chaos and evil that flourish in anarchy when we look at modern failed states, where there is no functioning government.[2] We also have seen many more examples of countries that have suffered under the grip of unjust laws, or laws unjustly applied. Fascism, communism, and dictatorships of the left and right all oppress their citizens.

Voluntary compliance is the gold standard for any legal system.

But enforcement is also needed, both to deter wrongdoing and to punish violators. A simple example: Speed limits are routinely ignored by motorists, but the use of speed cameras has had a noticeable, if temporary, effect, especially where it is followed up with traffic tickets and fines.[3]

Similarly, swift and certain punishment of violent offenders is important not only for justice, but also for its deterrence value. When others see that wrongdoers are punished, they are more likely to obey the law. However, we need to take the time to make sure the people we are punishing are really guilty. When we incarcerate the wrong people, or even the right people for the wrong reasons, we undermine the rule of law.

LOCKING UP THE PEOPLE WE'RE MAD AT

The United States is home to 5 percent of the world's population and 25 percent of the world's prisoners. Our rate of incarceration is five times the world average. Among rich countries we also have one of the highest murder rates. The good news is that our violent crime rate has been declining.[4] Some observers say that's because so many criminals have been locked up where they can't commit more crimes. But most of our prisoners are actually doing time for nonviolent offenses.

Craig DeRoche, former speaker of the Michigan House of Representatives and now senior vice president of Christian Fellowship, decries the lengthy mandatory minimum sentences that "ban federal judges from distinguishing between high-level and low-level, dangerous and nonviolent, or first-time and repeat offenders. Our prisons are full of nonviolent offenders we're just mad at, rather than violent people who truly need to be separated from society for a long time."[5]

The National Association of Evangelicals called for sentencing reform in a 1983 resolution. The NAE's call remains valid today:

> Dangerous criminals must be imprisoned to protect society. However, half of those in prison have been convicted of non-violent offenses. As an alternative or supplement to incarceration, Biblically-based sanctions, such as restitution, would benefit the victim of the crime and society in general, as well as help to rehabilitate the offender. Incidentally, the cost of this approach would be only a fraction of incarceration.[6]

More than half of inmates in state prisons have substance abuse disorders involving both drugs and alcohol, and 16 percent have serious mental illnesses.[7] Most of the mentally ill are nonviolent, but some do need intensive supervision. Treatment resources are woefully inadequate.

For most politicians, and particularly for prosecutors, chiefs of police, attorneys general, and others in law enforcement, being tough on crime has been a winning ticket. Voters are afraid of violent criminals and want them apprehended and locked up for as long as possible. In the 1990s, some states passed "three strikes" laws that mandated life imprisonment for a third conviction.[8] Other states passed harsh mandatory minimum sentences that prohibited judges from taking into account extenuating circumstances when determining the most appropriate punishment for a defendant.

The unintended consequences of getting tough on crime have been overcrowded prisons, unaffordable prison budgets, and lost opportunities to rehabilitate repentant offenders. There are also undoubtedly innocent people in prison who, facing the risk of decades behind bars and lacking good lawyers, chose to plea bargain and confess to an offense that they did not commit.

Restoring balance and sanity to our criminal laws has proven extraordinarily difficult. Politicians fear being considered "soft on crime" and particularly being blamed for a crime committed by someone whom they released from prison. The fear is not necessarily misplaced. In the 1988 presidential election, a controversial ad attacking Massachusetts Governor Michael Dukakis for granting weekend release to Willie Horton, a convicted murderer who later assaulted and raped a woman, gained nationwide attention. The attack suggested that someone who releases inmates from prison could not be trusted to keep us safe. More than two decades later, in a meeting to discuss criminal justice reform, one senator confided that the fear of another Willie Horton attack ad still keeps some of his colleagues from supporting sentencing reform.

If we're honest, some of us would prefer to "lock them up and throw away the key." But is that view informed by fear or faith? What does the Bible have to say about justice and jails?

CRIME AND PUNISHMENT IN THE BIBLE

You might be surprised at what the Bible teaches about crime. Genesis 3 presents Adam and Eve's fatal rebellion against God. Paul tells us that through this original sin, death spread to all people (Rom. 5:12). This did not take long: In Genesis 4 we learn of the first murder, when Adam and Eve's son Cain killed his brother Abel. Despite Cain's violence, God reached out to him, as he did to Adam and Eve. In his mercy, God did not execute Cain for his crime, but actually promised to protect him as he wandered in exile (Gen. 4:15–16).

Throughout the Bible there are accounts of crimes committed, though with relatively few examples of punishment. The Mosaic law contains over 600 laws, many with punishments prescribed for violations. But it is unclear how frequently the punishments were actually carried out.

Much more frequent are the accounts of unjust imprisonment. Joseph was sold into slavery and later wrongly accused of rape and imprisoned (Gen. 39). Daniel was thrown into the lion's den for praying to his God (Dan. 6). Jeremiah was kept in a muddy cistern because he told the truth about God's judgment (Jer. 37–38). John the Baptist was imprisoned for challenging King Herod on his immorality and was eventually beheaded (Mark 6:14–29). In the ultimate injustice, Jesus was crucified on false charges under Pontius Pilate.[9] Later, many of Jesus' followers were also imprisoned and some executed.

Quoting from Isaiah, Jesus declared in his first sermon that God had sent him "to proclaim freedom for the prisoners" (Luke 4:18). In Matthew 25:36, he directly identified with those in prison, saying, "I was in prison and you came to visit me."

The Bible also emphasizes the possibility of redemption of even the most hardened criminal. Moses, David, and Paul were all murderers rehabilitated into godly leaders. Matthew the tax collector—a white-collar criminal—became a disciple of Jesus and wrote one of the four Gospels (Matt. 9:9–13).[10] The thief on the cross could only manage a one-sentence sinner's prayer, but received the promise that he would be with Jesus in paradise (Luke 23:43). By God's grace, many who are in prison today have become followers of Jesus and now constitute what the NAE has called the "church-behind-the-walls."[11]

For those who are victims of crime, the Bible counsels forgiveness. Despite the enormity of the sins committed against him, Joseph found the strength to forgive his brothers and had the insight to see God's hand at work in his suffering (Gen. 45). "You intended to harm me," he told them truthfully, "but God intended it for good to accomplish what is now being done, the saving of many lives" (Gen. 50:20). In forgiving his brothers, Joseph not only blessed them, but also found healing for his own deep pain.

Jesus taught his followers to seek forgiveness and to forgive: "'Forgive us our debts, as we also have forgiven our debtors.'... For if you forgive other people when they sin against you, your heavenly Father will also forgive you. But if you do not forgive others their sins, your Father will not forgive your sins" (Matt. 6:12, 14–15). When Peter asked Jesus how often he should forgive, Jesus told him "not seven times, but seventy-seven times" (Matt. 18:22).

Jesus demonstrated the height and depth of forgiveness when he cried out from the cross, "Father, forgive them, for they do not know what they are doing" (Luke 23:34). Stephen, the first Christian martyr, echoed Jesus in his own final words as he was being stoned to death, "Lord, do not hold this sin against them" (Acts 7:60).

The biblical perspective should soften our hearts as we consider our response to those who are caught up in lives of crime. Do we need clear laws and consistent enforcement? Yes. Can families, churches, schools, and communities do more to prevent crime and steer our young people in the right direction? Certainly. Do people who have committed violent crimes and who are likely to do so again need to be incarcerated? Absolutely. But even there, when we have locked people into concrete cells for years or perhaps for life, we are called to visit them, to pray with them, and to point them to the Savior before whom we too have to kneel, crying, "Lord,... have mercy on us!" (Matt. 20:31).

VOTING FOR JUSTICE AND JAILS

Our leaders and candidates for office need to know that we support a well-conceived, well-run criminal justice system that keeps us safe, prevents crime, rehabilitates offenders, and restores victims. They should know that we are motivated, not by anger or fear, but by love (see 1 John 4:18).

Prison Fellowship has developed a helpful framework for what it calls "restorative justice." It places more emphasis on restoring the harmed party to wholeness, involving both the responsible party and the community. Government's role is to administer justice, not play the role of the aggrieved party.

Here are some areas of criminal justice policy that you should consider as you evaluate candidates' positions:

■ **Prevention.** Families, churches, schools, and other community institutions all play a role in raising our children to be productive, law-abiding citizens. Children who live with biological parents, attend good schools with caring teachers, and are involved in wholesome activities in their communities are far less likely to choose a life of crime. Police departments can help by establishing good relationships with the people in the communities they serve, treating all citizens with respect.

Policies and programs that strengthen families and communities will reduce the level of crime. Many churches reach out to the children of prisoners at Christmas time. Some have expanded to year-round ministries that provide love, support, and guidance to children and teens who desperately need it.

■ **Due process.** While on paper American citizens enjoy impressive legal protection, the quality of criminal investigation and prosecution varies widely. Low-income defendants are less likely to have the resources to defend their innocence. Bias against racial minorities remains a serious problem throughout our criminal justice system.[12] Prosecutors have the upper hand, and they sometimes take advantage of their position. We can make clear that we will not vote for sheriffs, prosecutors, and other law enforcement officials who abuse their power.

- **Sentencing.** Proper assessment is needed to determine the appropriate punishment. Legislators need to approve realistic and flexible sentencing guidelines that allow judges to do their job. The judge is the one person in our system who is charged with protecting the needs and rights of society, of the victim, and of the accused. We should not take away the judge's ability to judge. Judges should be creative in devising, wherever possible, sentences that repay rather than burden society and the victim.

- **Restitution.** When victims have lost property or other tangible goods, every effort should be made to restore them to wholeness. In the case of injury and death, this is often not possible, but there can still be compensation provided to the victim's family. This should come directly from the offender, wherever possible and appropriate, but should also be backed up with victim assistance funds allocated by the state. Where states are allowed to seize the assets of criminals or those who allow crimes to occur, these assets should be used to compensate victims, not pad the budgets of police departments—a practice that creates an incentive for abuse.[13]

- **Punishment.** Prisons should be designed to keep prisoners safe, provide opportunities for education and rehabilitation, and address the needs of those suffering from addiction or mental illness. The use of solitary confinement, which can cause serious mental health problems, should be strictly limited.[14] Prison wardens should be evaluated and rewarded according to their success in rehabilitating prisoners and the percentage of them who successfully reenter society. Good time credits should be offered to those who complete education or other programs that reduce their risk of recidivism. Family members should be able to visit regularly. Telephone service should be available at a reasonable cost for prisoners to be able to stay in touch with family members.[15]

- **Reentry.** Not every person who commits a violent crime will repent and one day become a Christian minister, as Billy Moore did. Some victims will be unwilling to reconcile, and some may need to be kept in prison for life. But most prisoners will one day complete their sentences and reenter society. How we treat them while they are in prison, and how we receive and support them when they come home, will have a lot to do with whether they rehabilitate or commit new offenses against society. Funding allocated for prisoner reentry will save money on future re-incarceration.[16]

Criminal justice can be a confusing issue to figure out. But voting on justice and jails doesn't have to be complicated. Ask these simple questions about the candidates who seek your support:

- Do they recognize the God-given dignity of every human being, both victims and perpetrators?

- Do they seek to restore both victims and offenders to wholeness?

- Do they appeal to voters' fears and anxieties or to a vision of justice and rehabilitation?

Consider this exhortation from the epistle to the Hebrews: "Continue to remember those in prison as if you were together with them in prison, and those who are mistreated as if you yourselves were suffering" (13:3). In context, this refers particularly to those who were wrongfully imprisoned for their faith. But recall that "while we were still sinners, Christ died for us" (Rom. 5:8). Keeping in mind our status as forgiven sinners may help us to vote for more justice and fewer jails.

Chapter 14

JOHN 3:16 AND FOREIGN POLICY

Thirty-two-year-old medical doctor Kent Brantly, along with his wife, Amber, and their two young children, left their Texas home in October 2013 and moved to Liberia, in war-torn West Africa. Brantly felt called by God to give two years of his life providing desperately needed medical care at the Eternal Love Winning Africa (ELWA) hospital in Monrovia, the capital city.

A few months later, as the deadly Ebola virus began spreading through Liberia and neighboring countries, Amber and the kids were evacuated back to Texas, but Kent stayed behind to continue serving in what had quickly become an international humanitarian crisis. The Centers for Disease Control warned that unless extraordinary measures were taken at great expense, as many as 1.4 million people could be infected within four months.[1] There was no vaccination and no known cure for the disease.

Despite rigorous precautions, Dr. Brantly became infected with the virus—the first American known to contract Ebola in the 2014 outbreak. Through a series of extraordinary interventions, Brantly received an experimental drug and was evacuated to the Emory University infectious disease center in Atlanta, Georgia. Thousands prayed. Brantly was treated and eventually recovered.

Thanks to the marvels of modern communications, Brantly's evacuation was widely reported, and millions of Americans became aware of his ordeal. *Time* magazine honored him as one of the five Ebola fighters named as Person of the Year.[2]

While most evangelical missionaries don't make the cover of *Time*, Brantly's story is far from unique. He follows more than a century of medical missionaries and humanitarians who have served in Africa, pioneering much of the modern medical work on the continent.[3]

Christian engagement in forgotten corners of the world has won the respect of noted *New York Times* columnist Nicholas Kristof, who wrote that "a disproportionate share of the aid workers I've met in the wildest places over the years, long after anyone sensible had evacuated, have been evangelicals, nuns and priests."[4]

Much of this evangelical humanitarian work is privately funded, but aid from Western countries has also played a significant role in advancing health services, often in partnership with religious missions and nonprofits. In responding to the Ebola crisis, for example, the U.S. Agency for International Development funded the work of many private agencies, including Samaritan's Purse, the evangelical agency that sponsored Dr. Brantly. This public-private partnership accomplished more than either government aid or private charity could achieve on their own.

It's easy to see why evangelicals support medical missionaries like Dr. Brantly. We care about people who are suffering, both physically and spiritually, and we reach out to them just as Jesus has taught us to do. Evangelicals have become aware and concerned about international issues in part because we know so many people who are living and working in other countries as missionaries or humanitarians. More than 1.5 million evangelicals actually travel overseas each year on short-term mission projects.[5]

We also know immigrants and refugees from other countries, because we have welcomed them into our churches and communities. For example, as many as 100,000 Liberians now live in the United States, and many of them belong to evangelical churches.[6] But why does our government get involved? What national interests are at stake? Liberia and the United States are separated by thousands of miles of the Atlantic Ocean. No direct flights connect our two countries, and we have no vital economic ties or military bases in Liberia.

Yet, an invisible virus illustrates how connected we are. The relative handful of Ebola cases seen in the United States in 2014, which caused disproportionate anxiety and even panic in some communities, were traced to West Africa. Viruses don't require visas and don't stop at international borders. Had Ebola spread as dramatically as was predicted, the risk of an Ebola outbreak in the United States would have sharply increased. We faced the choice of fighting Ebola in Africa, or waiting for it to reach our shores.

These connections can be multiplied as we zoom out from the specific case of Ebola and consider other threats to public health, as well as the potential for environmental disasters, terrorism, cyber warfare, forced migration, and the unthinkable risks of nuclear war. Any of these threats could profoundly impact our lives and our nation. As much as we may want to hunker down and focus on domestic concerns, this is an option our interconnected, globalized world doesn't afford us.

As Christians, we are drawn to engage with our global neighbors, motivated by God's love and the call to be witnesses to the gospel "to the ends of the earth" (Acts 1:8). We do this as part of our calling, whether supported or opposed by our government's foreign policy. But our international connections give us insights and concerns that warrant our engagement. As citizens, we want our country to play a constructive role in the world and to keep us safe. By voting for candidates who will implement wise foreign policy, including support for poverty-focused international assistance, we help secure a more peaceful, prosperous world, which helps us as well as our neighbors in Liberia and throughout the world.

FROM A CITY ON A HILL TO A GLOBAL VILLAGE

American foreign policy is closely linked with American identity. Shortly before landing in New England in 1630 with a small group of English Puritans, Captain John Winthrop told his passengers that the world would be watching them. He challenged them to be a model of Christian charity, following the prophet Micah's charge "to act justly and to love mercy and to walk humbly with your God" (6:8). They would be, he said, a city upon a hill, with the eyes of the world upon them.[7]

Winthrop's speech contains two ideas that have echoed throughout American history. On the one hand, he envisioned a community inwardly focused on establishing themselves in the New World. They had left England behind; they would not be returning. On the other hand, they were establishing a new political community that would be closely watched. They had, in some sense, a special mission to share with the world. Winthrop quoted from Moses' farewell address in Deuteronomy 30. Like the ancient Israelites, they were about to enter a new Promised Land, and by implication, they would be a blessing to the nations.

The vision of America's special place in the world can be seen in the Monroe Doctrine, which in 1823 declared the Western Hemisphere off limits to European powers.[8] It also led to the ideology of Manifest Destiny—which became a rationale for the westward expansion, a checkered history that includes conquest of Native American tribes and annexation of large parts of Mexico.[9] More recently, President John F. Kennedy and President Ronald

Reagan, among others, have used the "city on a hill" theme to articulate their vision of America's inspirational and leadership roles in the world.

Should our government even care about and try to influence what happens beyond our borders? Several reasons are offered for saying no. Some say that it is none of our business, that our overseas interventions unjustly impose our will and frequently make things worse. Others point to unresolved problems in our own country, and advocate letting other countries fend for themselves.

Supporters of a strong national defense advocate a muscular foreign policy that projects American power and influence throughout the world. In this view the world is a dangerous place, with foreign powers—and now terrorists—seeking to conquer or harm us. Only by maintaining a strong military and responding forcefully and even proactively to any threats can we assure our own safety and prosperity. The judgment of history, the advocates point out, has not been kind to appeasers, who buy peace today at the cost of greater threats tomorrow.

Interventionists also support active engagement, but with a broader agenda. Americans have built a unique nation blessed with freedom and prosperity. We should use our strength to promote our democratic and humanitarian values on behalf of oppressed and struggling people around the world. President George W. Bush's HIV/AIDS initiative is a good example of this. By making the world a better place, we benefit from greater security and economic growth. But more important, we will be standing up for our values and doing what is right.

Foreign policy realists believe the focus on values is often naïve. Rather than confronting dictators and demanding change, we should make deals even with our adversaries when doing so would advance our interests. Our interests include maintaining access to the commodities our economy needs, assuring markets for our exports, and containing or overthrowing any hostile powers that might threaten our security. We need not be squeamish about the company we keep. In fact, over time as the economies of oppressed countries improve, the people in these lands are likely to demand greater freedom and human rights.

Which perspective best describes your views on foreign policy? On what basis do you prefer this approach to the others?

UNITED? NATIONS

Following the upheavals of two world wars, world leaders met in San Francisco to approve the United Nations Charter, establishing a new international organization dedicated to maintaining international peace and security, developing friendly relations among nations, and facilitating cooperation in solving international problems.[10] The United Nations has not been popular among evangelicals. A strong bias against Israel, perceived threats to our national sovereignty, and an expensive, bureaucratic operating structure are some areas of concern. Evangelical publishing houses have produced books and films with fictional portrayals of the U.N. Secretary-General as the Antichrist. But for all its faults, the United Nations has enabled its nearly 200 member countries to work together in ways that would otherwise be difficult to achieve.[11]

The U.N. Universal Declaration of Human Rights, much like the Bill of Rights in the U.S. Constitution, establishes the equal dignity and worth of every person. Article 18 is particularly important, providing a strong statement on freedom of religion, including the right to change one's religion. This right, while far from being universally honored, provides the basis for appeals for change in countries that practice religious persecution.[12]

International treaties are important tools for establishing

agreements between nations on areas of common concern, such as the treatment of prisoners of war, the regulation of air and sea transport, nuclear nonproliferation, and the preservation of regions such as Antarctica. Critics often worry that ratifying treaties is a surrender of national sovereignty. There is concern that other countries will restrict our freedoms. While such concern is sometimes legitimate, treaties can also advance our national interests by securing the cooperation of other countries on issues of importance to us. As a nation committed to the rule of law, the United States benefits from clear rules of international conduct to which all countries can be held accountable.

BIBLICAL GUIDELINES

God is not an American. He is not necessarily on our nation's "side" in our dealings with other countries. In fact, if God did have a favorite nation, it was biblical Israel, which the prophet Zechariah referred to as "the apple of his eye" (Zech. 2:8).[13] We need political leaders who, like Abraham Lincoln, will say that "my concern is not whether God is on our side; my greatest concern is to be on God's side, for God is always right."[14]

Psalm 24:1 tells us that "The earth is the LORD's, and everything in it." God made everything and continues to oversee his creation. John 3:16 adds that "God so loved the world that he gave his one and only Son, that whoever believes in him shall not perish but have eternal life." Paul tells us in Philippians 2:11 that "every tongue" will confess Jesus Christ as Lord.

As Christians in America or China or Zimbabwe or any other country think about foreign policy, we do so first of all as members of God's multinational family.[15] Only within that context do we turn to the interests of our particular nation.

In Psalm 33 we find a powerful reflection on the nature and character of God and his dealings with the nations. While not specifically a psalm about foreign policy, it highlights important truths that should guide every nation. The United States, like all nations, will be judged by God's standards of justice and righteousness. Consider these qualities in Psalm 33 that should characterize every nation and its relations with other nations:

- **Integrity:** "For the word of the LORD is right and true; he is faithful in all he does" (v. 4). Does our nation honor its treaty obligations, keep its commitments, and deal honestly with other countries? Corruption is a big problem in governments and societies around the world, including in our own.[16] Various estimates put the annual cost of corruption as high as $500 billion to $1 trillion in lost productivity and wasted opportunities.[17]

- **Morality:** "The LORD loves righteousness and justice" (v. 5). These two closely related terms are characteristics of God, and they communicate what he requires of all people and nations, even those that do not profess to honor him. Paul tells us in Romans 1:18–20 that God has made his expectations clear in the very order of creation, so that all people (including us) are without excuse. Throughout the Bible we see examples of God judging the nations, such as Sodom and Gomorrah, Egypt, Assyria, Babylon, and the Canaanite tribes, as well as Israel itself.

  What God requires are not special religious rules, but basic moral concepts that are written on our heart and embedded in our conscience (Rom. 2:15). We need not be apologetic about insisting that our foreign policy, as with all of our government policies, upholds the basic standards of morality and truth that we know will promote human flourishing. The values that make a nation pleasing to God are those that our nation should promote internationally.

- **Religious freedom:** "Blessed is the nation whose God is the LORD" (v. 12). In a secular democracy, calling fellow citizens to turn to God is not the government's job. We don't want a government that commands worship of God at home or abroad. But our foreign policy should promote the freedom of people in all countries to respond to God according to their conscience and belief. Both the State Department and the independent U.S. Commission on International Religious Freedom publish annual reviews of religious freedom conditions around the world.[18]

- **Security:** "No king is saved by the size of his army; no warrior escapes by his great strength. A horse is a vain hope for deliverance; despite all its great strength it cannot save" (vv. 16–17). The warning against trusting in horses, a key source of military strength in ancient times, is repeated in Psalm 20:7: "Some trust in chariots and some in horses, but we trust in the name of the LORD our God."

  In a time when Israel's own stable of warhorses seemed insufficient, Isaiah warned against trusting in alliances with other military powers: "Woe to those who go down to Egypt for help, who rely on horses, who trust in the multitude of their chariots and in the great strength of their horsemen, but do not look to the Holy One of Israel, or seek help from the LORD" (31:1). The Egyptians, said Isaiah, are no match for God. When God acts against the Egyptians, "those who help will stumble, those who are helped will fall; all will perish together" (v. 3).

  Supporting a strong national defense is not at all inconsistent with trust in God. However, if we rely on our military strength and use that power to get our way in

149

world affairs, we are venturing into risky territory. Military power or superior weapons alone do not guarantee success. Witness the backlash to the use of drones in the struggle against terrorism, or the uselessness of nuclear weapons in any battle that we ourselves hope to survive.[19]

■ **Peace:** Christians are instructed by Paul in 1 Timothy 2:1–2 to pray for our leaders so that "we may live peaceful and quiet lives in all godliness and holiness." Most Christians have embraced the principles of "just war theory," which acknowledges the legitimacy of going to war in certain limited contexts.[20] Others believe that nations should never go to war, or at least that Christians should never participate in military conflict, a position known as pacifism. Still others embrace a theory of "just peacemaking" that some describe as a middle way. Whichever ethical framework we embrace, the goal of our foreign policy should be to establish and maintain peaceful relations and to resolve differences through negotiations wherever possible.[21]

As the world's most powerful nation, the United States plays a critical role in resolving disputes between other nations. We have extraordinary convening power, with diplomatic, economic, and military resources that can help pressure warring parties to negotiate. Resolving international conflicts helps us as well as other countries. Wars cause civilian and military deaths, produce refugees, disrupt trade, and destabilize alliances. These effects don't stop at international borders.

To take an extreme example, consider the possibility of a nuclear war between India and Pakistan, two nations that have had uneasy relations for years. By some estimates, even a small-scale nuclear exchange between these two countries located thousands of miles away from the United States could lead to a global famine that would threaten the lives of two billion people—more than a quarter of the world's population.[22] Our own country would be deeply impacted by such an unimaginable tragedy.

In an age of terrorism we need to be concerned not only about countries, but also about other groups that pose a threat to peace. Our foreign policy needs to address the roots of terrorism without inadvertently creating new terrorists who are angry at our anti-terrorism interventions.

■ **Meeting human needs.** "But the eyes of the LORD are on those who fear him, on those whose hope is in his unfailing love, to deliver them from death and keep them alive in famine" (Ps. 33:18–19). God used the Egyptian government under Joseph's leadership to avert widespread famine, and God continues to work through governments today to accomplish his purposes.

Over the past three millennia much has been learned about weather patterns, agricultural methods, and food security strategies. A Famine Early Warning System enables world leaders to predict with increasing accuracy where food shortages are likely to occur.[23] To our shame, we often ignore these warnings, leading to needless loss of life. Even sudden onset disasters, such as earthquakes and hurricanes, are known to occur most frequently in certain regions of the world. Wise building codes and other regulations can prevent much loss, and relief supplies can be prepositioned in the areas likeliest to experience disasters.

In a world economy marked by vast disparities in wealth and income, wealthy countries have both an interest and an obligation to help poorer countries grow their economies, develop their people, and address humanitarian crises. Wise trade agreements can help. Early on, in Genesis 4, we see labor diversification with animal husbandry, agriculture, music, and toolmaking all mentioned. Trade allows people to do what they do best, develop their God-given potential, and exchange the fruits of their labor with others.

Critics of trade agreements often cite projected job losses as imports substitute for domestic goods and services. Of course, a job lost in one country may represent one or more jobs gained in another country. And if the trade agreement leads to increased exports, there will also be new jobs created at home. The best evidence suggests that trade has relatively little net impact on the number of jobs, but has a positive impact on average wages.

Beyond the economic issues, critics point out that if trading partners do not have comparable health, labor, or environmental standards, the net effect of trade may be to move production to the location with the lowest standards. For this reason, trade agreements often include provisions addressing those issues, so that trade is not only free, but fair.

AMBASSADORS FOR CHRIST

One of the first actions every Christian voter can take regarding foreign policy issues is to become better informed about the world beyond our borders. In addition to reading widely, take advantage of opportunities to get to know people from other countries and other religions, whether in your own community or by traveling. World Relief, the humanitarian arm of the NAE, connects volunteers with specific refugee families.[24] Could you host such a family and in the process become a better-informed voter on foreign policy issues? You could also support a missionary family and learn more about the country where they serve. Some of us can learn another language, which provides a unique window on the world.

This is also the time to remember that we too have a diplomatic mission: as Christians, we are ambassadors for God (2 Cor. 5:20). Ambassadors represent the one who sent them. When they face opposition, they utilize a whole range of diplomatic skills to establish rapport with those they seek to influence. We can do the same as we represent our Lord.

On some occasions private American citizens may be able to contribute to better relationships with other countries through the connections we establish with their citizens. This is known as Track Two diplomacy.[25] (Track One is what our official ambassadors do.) In 2014, at the invitation of the State Department, I (Leith) joined a Catholic cardinal and a Muslim imam to travel to the Central African Republic during a time of civil war. We met with local evangelical, Catholic, and Muslim leaders to encourage them to work together to stop the fighting.

As you consider voting for presidential and congressional candidates, ask to what extent each candidate would uphold the values of integrity, morality, freedom, security, peace, and meeting human needs. Do they exhibit these qualities in their own lives? Do they have relevant international experience? What have they learned from that? Do they speak respectfully of other countries, or do they resort to narrow nationalism? Have they bothered to learn another language? And do they support religious freedom globally so that your Christian brothers and sisters can worship freely?

As you follow world events on the news and through your international relationships, pray regularly for your leaders and for those affected by wars, disasters, and oppression. Let your elected representatives know of your foreign policy concerns. And in your own world, share God's love and be ambassadors for Christ with all those God sends your way.

Chapter 15

CREATION CARE

Taking a fall drive through New England as the leaves are changing, standing at the edge of the Grand Canyon, or gazing at Niagara Falls, it's easy to appreciate the stunning beauty and majestic power of God's creation. As Psalm 19:1 states, "The heavens declare the glory of God; the skies proclaim the work of his hands." The Swedish composer Karl Gustav Boberg captured our sentiments well in his famous hymn "How Great Thou Art":

> *O Lord my God, when I in awesome wonder*
> *Consider all the worlds Thy hands have made,*
> *I see the stars, I hear the rolling thunder,*
> *Thy power throughout the universe displayed:*
> *Then sings my soul, my Savior God, to Thee,*
> *How great Thou art! How great Thou art!*
>
> *When through the woods and forest glades I wander*
> *And hear the birds sing sweetly in the trees,*
> *When I look down from lofty mountain grandeur,*
> *And hear the brook and feel the gentle breeze:*
> *Then sings my soul, my Savior God, to Thee,*
> *How great Thou art! How great Thou art!*

On the other hand, absorbing the sights and smells of a garbage dump or coughing at the polluted air of an industrial city graphically highlights the consequences of failing to responsibly steward God's world.

God's creation is breathtaking when seen in the intricacy of God's design, much of which we do not yet understand. Astronomers continue to explore the reaches of space, oceanographers survey the oceans, biologists discover new species—and the more they study, the more they realize how little they know or understand.

Damage to God's creation, too, can go beyond what is visible to the naked eye. Pollution of our land, air, and water leads to illness and death. Changes to our climate have, according to scientists, already destroyed habitats, acidified the ocean, melted polar ice caps, and increased the severity of storms, floods, forest fires, and droughts. Our reserves of fertile agricultural land, fresh water, and mineral resources are being depleted. These issues have been chronicled extensively; a good place to learn more is the Evangelical Environmental Network's website, www.creationcare.org.

There is also good news. Our votes, as well as our actions as individuals and as a nation, make a difference. The first national legislation on air quality, the Air Pollution Control Act, was signed into law by President Dwight D. Eisenhower in 1955. A major advance came in 1970 when President Richard Nixon signed the National Environmental Policy Act, creating the Environmental Protection Agency (EPA) and the Clean Air Act. During its first two decades, the Clean Air Act is estimated to have saved 200,000 lives and prevented millions of debilitating illnesses.[1] In 1990 President George H. W. Bush approved major amendments to the Clean Air Act that have saved an estimated 160,000 additional lives and further improved the health of millions of Americans.[2] When we work together, we are able to clean up what we have polluted.

Much has also been accomplished to restore the quality of our nation's lakes and rivers. Industrial pollution on the Cuyahoga

River in Ohio was so bad that the river actually caught on fire thirteen times. A 1912 fire killed five people, and a major fire in 1952 caused $1.3 million in damages.[3] In 1972 Congress passed the Clean Water Act, which regulated raw sewage and other pollutants that had previously been regularly dumped into our rivers and lakes. Today our rivers and lakes are much cleaner than before, although more needs to be done.

The Aspen Institute notes several positive actions that our nation has taken over the past four decades to improve public health, including banning DDT, reducing acid rain, removing lead from gasoline, restricting secondhand tobacco smoke, improving vehicle efficiency and emissions controls, regulating toxic wastes, and cleaning up our waterways.[4]

While private actions and market forces played a role in these achievements, they would not have occurred without supporting legislation and regulation. We can thank politicians in both parties for their efforts. Of course, politicians acted because ordinary citizens urged and even pressured them to do so.

Voters who are concerned about caring for God's creation need to continue pushing for well-designed laws and regulations that will enable us to meet the new challenges we face in the twenty-first century. If we want our political leaders to lead, we need to support them. And if they won't lead, we need to find leaders who will. But first, let's see what the Bible has to say about God's plans for his creation.

THE BIBLICAL PLAN OF CREATION

The Bible teaches that God made all things, including the stars, sun, and moon; the oceans and continents of earth; the air that we breathe; and the amazing variety of life, including humans, plants, and animals. Humans appear tiny and insignificant when seen against the backdrop of the vast universe with more stars than we can count. The psalmist exclaimed, "When I consider your heavens, the work of your fingers, the moon and the stars, which you have set in place, what is mankind that you are mindful of them, human beings that you care for them?" (Ps. 8:3–4). The answer is that humans have a special place in God's creation: "You made them a little lower than the angels and crowned them with glory and honor" (v. 5).

God is pleased when we take time to delight in his creation. Whether we visit one of our magnificent national parks, or simply admire what grows in our backyard, or vote for leaders who help preserve this beauty, we honor God by appreciating and protecting what he has made.

The Bible does not say that the world was made "for" us to use as we see fit. To the contrary, we and all other creatures were made for God, to bring him glory. Our treatment of creation must reflect our Creator's love and care for his handiwork, in ways that honor him.

This doesn't mean that we shouldn't work to control invasive species or pests that threaten human life. Eradication of mosquitoes in some African villages has saved countless lives by preventing malaria. But even here we should be cautious in light of possible unintended consequences of our actions in a complex ecosystem. Our sinful rebellion has brought a curse on the land that makes our work—including our political efforts to establish and maintain God-honoring creation care policies—more challenging (see Gen. 3:17).

Genesis 2:15 tells us that God placed Adam in the garden of Eden "to work it and take care of it." When sin entered the world, it created tension in this two-part assignment to tend and protect the garden. Working the land, for example, produces food that feeds the billions who now live on our planet. But it can deplete the soil, threatening future productivity, and pollute the water-ways, especially when soil erodes or pesticides are used improperly. Large-scale agriculture helps feed the planet, but also disrupts wildlife habitats.

Other aspects of a modern economy, such as mining and man-ufacturing, have contributed to major advances in our quality of life. But they also take a toll, even when pursued responsibly, rais-ing concerns about the sustainability of our current practices. This is part of the tension of living in a fallen world.

ALL GOD'S CREATURES

At each stage in the Genesis creation story, God reviewed his work and saw that it was "good" (Gen. 1:4, 10, 12, 18, 21, 25). Each aspect of God's creation is valuable in its own right. At the end of the process, when God saw *all* that he had made, he pronounced the whole "very good" (v. 31). God made the various aspects of cre-ation interdependent and interconnected, so that they fully achieve their God-given purpose together, bringing glory to God, when each one is in place and doing its part.[5]

The well-known story of Noah shows the importance God placed on animals by making room for them in the ark (Gen. 6–9). Animals are frequently mentioned throughout the Bible. There are more than 450 references to cattle and 400 references to sheep.[6] Animals are important in their own right, as well as for their essen-tial contribution to the survival of human beings.

In Job 38–39, the longest biblical passage dealing with non-human creation, we see a collection of exquisite nature poems describing the sea, the dawn, the deep (underworld), light, dark-ness, snow, hail, lightning, wind, rain, thunderstorms, dew, stars, clouds, lions, ravens, mountain goats, deer, wild donkeys, wild oxen, ostriches, warhorses, hawks, and eagles. These verses imaginatively describe the diverse aspects of God's creation. The poetry matches the artistry seen in what they describe.

Nature and animals are important to God quite apart from any apparent usefulness to humans. Eloquent in their own right, the poems are also God's surprising answer, in his own words, to Job's questions about his suffering. The poems help Job refocus from his own struggles to delighting with God in his handiwork. As we think about our place in God's creation, we should remember that we share the world with the amazing diversity of God's creation, which he loves and cares for. When we care for creation, we are actually imitating God our heavenly Father.

Psalm 104 is an eloquent hymn celebrating the diversity of God's creation and providential care. It moves from the cosmic—setting the earth on its foundations (v. 5)—to a joyful celebration of wild donkeys, birds, cattle, cedar trees, pine trees, storks, wild goats, coneys (rock badgers), and lions. "All creatures look to you to give them their food at the proper time. When you give it to them, they gather it up; when you open your hand, they are satisfied with good things" (vv. 27–28). The psalmist promises, "I will sing to the LORD all my life; I will sing praise to my God as long as I live" (v. 33).

The intimate connection between humans and the rest of creation is highlighted in Paul's letter to the Romans, where he wrote:

> The creation waits in eager expectation for the children of God to be revealed. For the creation was subjected to frustration, not by its own choice, but by the will of the one who subjected it, in hope that the creation itself will be liberated from its bondage to decay and brought into the glorious freedom of the children of God.
>
> We know that the whole creation has been groaning as in the pains of childbirth right up to the present time. Not

only so, but we ourselves, who have the firstfruits of the Spirit, groan inwardly as we wait eagerly for our adoption to sonship, the redemption of our bodies (Rom. 8:19–23).

In this passage Paul refers to the creation four times, telling us of its eager expectation, its frustration, its hopes for liberation, and its groans of pain. This suggests a reference to the effects of human sin, the curse on the ground that followed Adam's sin (Gen. 3:17–19). Creation groans under the weight of human sin, which includes willful damage to what God has created.

Due to our interconnectedness, we humans groan too. Our attempts to elect leaders who will guide us in the care of God's creation, like our efforts to establish peace and justice among people, have had mixed results. There have been remarkable successes, as noted above, but also continuing failures, including the extinction of many species, poor management of fresh water supplies, and ineffective cleanup of toxic waste sites. For that reason, both humans and nonhuman creation eagerly await the redemption—which has begun, but has not been revealed in its fullness.

Some have taken Paul's talk about futility to suggest we shouldn't even try to relieve the suffering of creation. But to wait eagerly doesn't mean to sit back and do nothing. We all know that we will eventually die, but when we get sick, we go to the doctor, have surgery, and take medicine in order to lessen our pain and improve our health. Our vision of freedom and the coming glory should spur us to do all that we can to stop misusing God's creation and to reverse past harm. This is certainly in our best interest—and a way of honoring our Creator. We have the Spirit empowering us and guiding us. We should demonstrate our love for God and neighbor by supporting leaders who will exercise responsible stewardship of his creation.

In his letter to the Colossians Paul provides the clearest New Testament picture of Jesus Christ's relationship to his creation:

The Son is the image of the invisible God, the firstborn over all creation. For in him all things were created: things in heaven and on earth, visible and invisible, whether thrones or powers or rulers or authorities; all things have been created through him and for him. He is before all things, and in him all things hold together. And he is the head of the body, the church; he is the beginning and the firstborn from among the dead, so that in everything he might have the supremacy. For God was pleased to have all his fullness dwell in him, and through him to reconcile to himself all things, whether things on earth or things in heaven, by making peace through his blood, shed on the cross (Col. 1:15–20).

Christ is called here the "firstborn over all creation." This does not mean that he was created, but that he is intimately connected with his creation. While not a created being, he is one of us. He is supreme over all things, and he exercises his supremacy in self-giving love through his sacrificial death on the cross.

The comprehensive and repeated reference to "all things" shows us that his focus extends beyond humans to the glorious mission of reconciling every aspect of creation to himself. He is interested not only in us, but in everything that he has made. As God's redeemed people, we come to share in Christ's love and care for all of creation.

At the end of the book of Revelation, John offers a glimpse of the new heaven and new earth that will be revealed when the work of redemption is complete. It will be a glorious time of direct communion with God, without tears, death, mourning, crying, or pain. Everything will be made new (Rev. 21:1–5). Some have taken John's vision to mean that we are free to use God's creation as we see fit, since God will soon be remaking everything anyway. But that misses the point of John's revelation. God's creation will be made new, not replaced. What we do now, including how we vote, matters.

Or to put it more simply, if God created it, why would we will-fully damage it or not do our best to protect it? To Christians, this is not merely a political issue, but a spiritual one as well.

LOVE OUR NEIGHBORS NOW AND THEN

At least seventy-five Bible verses instruct about relationships among neighbors, including ten direct commands to "love your neigh-bor."[7] One way we love our neighbors is by taking care of the world that we share with them, by not polluting it and by conserving the natural resources that are necessary for life. Our support for sound creation care policies helps us to love our current neighbors, both next door and around the world. Caring for creation is particularly a way of loving our neighbors who are living in poverty. It is the poorest people in the world who are most vulnerable to famine, floods, droughts, pollution, and other threats.[8]

We can also love future neighbors by taking good care of God's world and leaving it for succeeding generations in at least as good a condition as we received it. God's blessings were prom-ised, for example, not only to Abraham, but also to his descendants (Gen. 17:7).

The Bible is realistic about human greed and selfishness. So, in addition to commands for voluntary charity for those in need, it also prescribes laws that regulated relations among neighbors in ancient Israel. For example, sharing agricultural produce was required, but also restricted: "If you enter your neighbor's vine-yard, you may eat all the grapes you want, but do not put any in your basket. If you enter your neighbor's grainfield, you may pick kernels with your hands, but you must not put a sickle to their standing grain" (Deut. 23:24–25). We need laws as well as gener-ous hearts to provide for conditions in which the interests of both current and future generations are protected. And of course, we need wise leaders to make and implement just laws.

HOW THEN SHALL WE VOTE?

Out of love for Christ, along with concern for our own survival, we should vote for leaders who support legislation and policies that will care for God's creation. We need leaders who will take seriously our responsibilities to care for the earth and all its inhabitants. Ask candidates what they would do to lead their city, state, or nation to maintain clean air, water, and shelter; to safeguard the supplies of minerals, metals, energy, and other resources; and to protect endangered species and ecosystems, both for us and for future generations.

In light of our biblical responsibilities, here are some policy goals that we can ask our leaders to support. There are different ways of accomplishing these goals. Part of the discernment task is to figure out which approaches are most likely to achieve the desired goals with the fewest collateral consequences.

- **Clean air.** Maintain air that is healthy and free from pollutants.

- **Clean water.** Keep our water supplies free of dangerous chemicals. Regulate the use of agricultural and industrial chemicals that pollute our waterways. Promote water conservation and recycling.

- **Clean energy.** Promote efforts to reduce pollution from current energy sources and to develop clean energy sources that don't pollute. Adjust incentives in the tax code to shift investment from fossil fuels to renewable energy sources.

- **Humane treatment of animals.** Enforce laws prohibiting animal abuse. Encourage respectful treatment of animals by farmers, ranchers, and breeders.

- **Species diversity.** Protect habitats for wild animals. Strengthen protection of endangered species. Preserve the ecosystems we all depend on.

- **Prepare for climate disruptions.** Increase emergency preparedness for the heat waves, extreme cold, floods, droughts, and forest fires that may become more intense in coming years. Reduce the amount of heat-trapping carbon and methane released into the atmosphere. Enforce building codes in storm-prone zones and along the coasts.

- **Promote international cooperation.** Ecological catastrophes don't stop at national borders. What happens in other countries affects us, and vice versa. The United States has much to share about how to clean up air and water and address other issues. We should share our expertise and learn from others. For example, Israel has pioneered the use of drip irrigation and now recycles most of its waste water.[9] We can learn from them.

- **Protect our parks and open spaces.** Whether we live in cities, suburbs, or rural areas, all Americans should have opportunities to enjoy the natural splendor of God's creation.

Some of these policies are best implemented at the national level, others at the state or local level. Where possible, market-based solutions should be considered, which disperse power rather than concentrating it in government. Regulations that allow flexibility in using a variety of means to achieve a desired goal would promote efficient protection of our land, air, and water with the least economic impact. For example, the Clean Power Plan establishes goals for each state's carbon emissions and allows the states to decide which of several strategies to use to meet those goals. States can also work together in regional alliances to achieve greater reductions in pollution at a lower cost.[10]

These recommendations will strike some as inadequate and others as overly aggressive. What is politically possible may fall short of what is needed. Creation care is sometimes pitted against jobs and economic growth, as if we could prosper without a healthy natural world. Both are necessary for human flourishing. Both are part of a faithful response to God.

Some say we can't afford to care for God's creation. But can we afford not to? If you don't change the oil in your car, you will eventually have expensive repair bills. If we don't care for God's creation, we will also pay a high price in human life and health, as well as in the long-term sustainability of our economy.

Don't let the perfect be the enemy of the good. Find and support leaders who understand our responsibility to care for the earth and its creatures, who can clearly and convincingly explain what needs to change, and who have the courage to lead our cities, states, and nation in the direction of an abundant, sustainable future in harmony with all God's creation.

God has given us a wonderful world to care for and enjoy. As Christians we should take the lead in protecting our Father's world. When we vote for leaders who will preserve our natural inheritance for the enjoyment of our own and future generations, we honor our Creator. As we embrace the privilege of stewarding God's creation, we are invited to put our hope in God, "who richly provides us with everything for our enjoyment" (1 Tim. 6:17). And as we are generous and faithful in our lives and in our voting, we lay "a firm foundation for the coming age" and "take hold of the life that is truly life" (v. 19). What a great invitation!

Chapter 16

DEALING WITH DIFFERENCES AND DISAGREEMENTS

Sometimes your perspective makes all the difference. A French citizen who became a British subject was asked what his change of nationality meant. "Yesterday, the Battle of Waterloo was a defeat," he replied. "Today, the Battle of Waterloo was a victory."

Of course, differences in perspective can be consequential. For example, when you encounter an unplanned and possibly unwanted pregnancy, do you think more about the impact on the parents or about the developing baby? Do you approach the issue of criminal justice from the perspective of a potential crime victim or of someone who could be falsely accused and at the mercy of a biased jury? When you discuss immigration policy, do you think more about an American who might face extra competition for a job, about an immigrant family with hopes and dreams for a better life, or about an employer struggling to find good workers?

Each perspective suggests different emphases and priorities. It's easy to see how differences of perspective can become heated disagreements and even bitter conflicts. How a society handles these conflicts says a lot about its character, values, and health.

CELEBRATING A CIVIL SOCIETY

Alexis de Toqueville famously analyzed the vibrancy of American civil society in his classic work, *Democracy in America*. He noted the vital role played by nongovernmental organizations, voluntarily founded and supported by concerned American citizens.

American civil society continues to be robust in the twenty-first century. We have more than 1.5 million registered nonprofit organizations, including churches, clubs, charities, coalitions, schools, hospitals, and advocacy groups.[1] The range of topics is mind-boggling, from Alcoholics Anonymous to the Zoroastrian Society of North Texas. Thanks to the marvels of modern communications, each group can have a website, a Facebook page, an email list, blogs, newsletters, and other publications, all inexpensively produced and disseminated. Groups with lots of money can do even more. Many of the groups have ideas and positions on public policy questions. This leads to a robust public square, but also a lot of disagreements.

Some of the issues on which Americans disagree include abortion, affirmative action, capital punishment, climate change, debt and deficits, gun control, immigration, marriage, nuclear weapons, sexual orientation, taxes, and war. These disagreements touch on core issues of values, of right and wrong, of life and death. Some advocacy organizations promote extreme views on different sides. It's hard to have a civil conversation or debate with the other side once they have been labeled "The Enemy."

By giving energy, time, and attention to their one issue, the minority who are true believers often have an outsized impact on the debate. The majority do not even pay close attention to the debate, unless a crisis or celebrity pushes the issue into the headlines. When they do stop and think about the issue, many Americans typically find themselves somewhere in the muddled middle.

As the number of viewpoints being expressed has increased, so has the level of disagreement. But individuals are able to tune out messages they don't want to hear, and they listen only to ideas with which they already agree. This is sometimes referred to as an echo chamber. Each group in its isolated silo tends to become more confirmed and one-sided in what it believes, with little chance to consider other viewpoints. When it does encounter contrary opinions, the exchange can quickly become testy. Instead of a civil debate, we often witness personal attacks on motives or character. This happens in church as well as in politics.

HOW TO DEAL WITH POLITICAL DIFFERENCES BIBLICALLY

It is easy to get caught up in the uncharitable rhetoric, intransigence, and tunnel vision that divide our nation, but our faith offers us a better way. The Bible offers instructions on how to handle disagreements, and it gives examples, good and bad, of how conflict was handled. We can learn from both.

COOPERATION AND CONSCIENTIOUS OBJECTION

Exiled in Babylon, Daniel and his young Hebrew friends faced a dilemma when they were selected for service in the administration of the pagan king Nebuchadnezzar. This was a great opportunity, considering the alternatives. They were willing to serve, but did not want to defile themselves with a diet that their faith forbade them to eat. They were in no position to bargain, but Daniel used his keen diplomatic skills to negotiate a ten-day trial period in which they would eat only kosher vegetables. It worked.

We can learn from Daniel's example. Rather than just complaining about a politician or policy you don't like, look for those proposing creative alternatives that could win broader support. Getting politicians to change their mind, or getting a law or regulation changed, is usually not easy, but that shouldn't stop us from trying. Support candidates who work with opponents to identify win/win solutions whenever possible. Be open to new approaches, as long as they don't compromise fundamental principles.

Later, when Daniel was forbidden to pray to his God, there was no room for compromise. He stood, or perhaps better, knelt on his principles and accepted the consequence of being thrown into the lion's den. God honored his faith and preserved his life. There are times when we may be asked to violate our conscience or beliefs, and no win/win solution appears possible. Even here, we should first pray and ask God what our faith actually requires in this situation.

Daniel's friends likewise refused to bow down to the golden image and were thrown into the fiery furnace. They too were saved, but they did not know in advance that they would be. They told the king that they would obey their God even if he chose not to save them from the fire. This is uncompromising faith at its finest. Their witness continues to inspire all who hear their story, even as it provides a model for how we should disagree with our government: Respectfully negotiate when we can; stand on principle when we can't, but accept the consequences.

Some areas where conscientious objection has been accommodated to a limited extent in American law include excusing pacifists from military service, pro-life nurses from helping with abortions, and clergy who object to participating in social security. For example, some Christians believe their faith forbids them to serve in the military. If these citizens are drafted, they can go through the process of applying for conscientious objector status and serve in a noncombatant role. Some who oppose even noncombatant service have chosen instead to serve time in jail.

Christians may disagree on debatable issues, as in the biblical case of eating meat offered to idols (see 1 Cor. 10:27–31). In these cases, Christians should look for ways to live peacefully with their neighbors and with one another, as Paul counseled: "If it is possible, as far as it depends on you, live at peace with everyone" (Rom. 12:18).

PROPHETIC WITNESS AND DENUNCIATION

Not all prophets were as diplomatic as Daniel. Amos referred to the Samaritan women who oppressed the poor as cows who would be taken away on meat hooks (Amos 4:1–2). John the Baptist called his listeners a "brood of vipers" (Luke 3:7), and Jesus himself called the scribes and Pharisees "hypocrites" and "whitewashed tombs" (Matt. 23:27). James warned rich people of the coming misery: "Your wealth has rotted, and moths have eaten your clothes. Your gold and silver are corroded. Their corrosion will testify against you and eat your flesh like fire" (James 5:2–3).

There may be a place for this kind of language in our public witness. Modern prophets may jolt our society into awareness of sin. Martin Luther King Jr. inspired the nation with his dream of all God's children being "free at last." But he also challenged the nation, and the church, for its complacency in the face of continued racial injustice. In his classic work "Letter from a Birmingham Jail," he wrote that "injustice anywhere is a threat to justice everywhere."[2] He went on to name and detail the effects of racism: the humiliation and "stinging darts" of segregation, police brutality, home and church bombings, and the economic oppression that left millions "smothering in an airtight cage of poverty." King did not mince words.

However, we sometimes forget that each of the biblical prophets, like King, also brought a message of hope as well as the offer of forgiveness if the listeners repented. Isaiah prophesied judgment, but also promised that "those who hope in the LORD will renew their strength" (40:31) and "you will go out in joy and be led forth in peace" (55:12). We should ask if we yearn for our listeners to repent, or if, like Jonah, we may resent God for his mercy and grace on those whom we see as undeserving (Jonah 4:1–2).

UNITY IN DIVERSITY

In the Acts of the Apostles, Luke tells the story of the church growing amid opposition from both religious and political leaders. There was excitement and unity at the beginning, when "all the believers were one in heart and mind" (Acts 4:32; see also 2:44). That is surely a good goal for followers of Jesus in any age.

When challenged by the religious authorities, the apostles respectfully but firmly stood their ground, explaining that "we cannot help speaking about what we have seen and heard" (Acts 4:20), and "we must obey God rather than human beings!" (5:29). The external opposition may have actually strengthened their internal unity. Recent challenges to religious liberty in the United States have similarly brought Christians together across denominational and other divides.

But Luke leaves no doubt about the real tensions and disagreements that arose within the young Christian community. Acts 5 contains the chilling confrontation with Ananias and Sapphira over lying to the community. They didn't get a second chance. Chapter 6 reveals ethnic tensions between Greek and Hebrew believers. The Greek widows were being overlooked in the food distribution. This conflict was resolved by the appointment of deacons, all Greek, to create a new balance of power within the community. Some of our racial and ethnic tensions in both church and society would be lessened if we followed this example of power sharing and deferring to the leadership of those who have been excluded.

POLICY AND THEOLOGY DISPUTES

The newly converted Saul of Tarsus was initially rejected by the Jerusalem believers due to his past offenses. It took an intervention from Barnabas to achieve reconciliation (Acts 9:19–30). Peter encountered criticism for changing his views on what was required of Gentile believers (11:1–18). This led to a "sharp dispute and debate" between Paul and Barnabas on the one side (15:2, 36–41), and Judean church leaders on the other (vv. 1–21).

The conflict was both deep seated and important to resolve, so the church leaders called their first major church council in Jerusalem. After much debate, a compromise agreement was reached. Neither side got everything it wanted, but they found a solution that all could live with. This created a working agreement that served the church during its formative years. Note that this agreement was not permanent: Most Gentile believers today accept the prohibition on sexual immorality, but not the dietary restrictions imposed by this first ecumenical church council.

However, resolving this major church policy question did not bring an end to conflicts.

Paul and Barnabas, who were on the same side in the dispute about rules for Gentiles, disagreed about whom to take with them on their next missionary journey (Acts 15:36–41). They had "such a sharp disagreement" that they parted company, each recruiting a new companion to replace the other (v. 39). Agreement on principles and policies is a good start, but we shouldn't be surprised when we still have to deal with conflicts over personal or personnel differences. This is where Paul's call to "be devoted to one another in brotherly love" and "honor one another above yourselves" (Rom. 12:10) must guide both our hearts and our minds.

JUDGMENT CALLS

In Acts 19 we see Paul again in conflict with his disciples and the local authorities, who disagreed with his desire to address a riotous crowd in Ephesus. On this occasion Paul relented, but in chapter 21, when he disclosed his risky plan to go to Jerusalem, against the advice of his companions, he would not listen to their counsel. We can read about what happened next, but we can't know what might have occurred, for better or worse, if Paul had listened to the advice of his friends.

As voters, too, we have to make judgment calls, which our friends may or may not support. We should listen to the ideas and opinions of others, but in the end, how we vote and what positions we take on issues should be based on our own prayer and discernment of God's leading. The crowd, like political parties and candidates, is sometimes wrong.

FACTIONALISM AND RECONCILIATION

Paul's first letter to the Corinthians reveals deep conflict in one of the churches he founded and served. The church in Corinth was divided into several factions (1 Cor. 1:12; 3:4). The existence of jealousy and quarreling, said Paul, were signs of immaturity and worldliness (3:3). Likewise, their failure to amicably resolve conflicts outside of the secular court system tarnished their Christian witness (6:6).

Paul's prescription for the divided Corinthians was threefold. First, they should absorb and forgive the wrong that was done to them, rather than inflict it on others—even their own brothers in the faith (6:7–8). Second, rather than making their differences a source of division, they should use their diverse gifts to build up one another in a spirit of love (chaps. 12–13). Third, they should turn their focus outward and think about people who are worse off than they are, in this case the poor and persecuted believers in Jerusalem. Paul instructed the Corinthians to contribute weekly to the Jerusalem relief fund (16:1–4).

In Paul's second letter to the Corinthians he wrote about the ministry of reconciliation that God has given those who have themselves been reconciled to God through Christ (2 Cor. 5:18–19). Paul testified that the experience of being forgiven by God enabled him to endure great hardship on their behalf (6:5–10). Rather than insisting on his rights, he was able to freely sacrifice on behalf of others. In the political context this tells us that we should not be concerned only for our own rights and needs, but also for the rights and needs of others.

AVOIDING ENTANGLING ALLIANCES

Paul warned the Corinthians not to lose their distinctiveness by being "yoked together with unbelievers" (2 Cor. 6:14). This verse is often taken as a prohibition against marrying an unbeliever. Such an application is warranted, although it is likely not what Paul had in mind in this passage. The Greek word translated "yoked together" suggests an alliance of two unequal partners who have contradictory commitments.

In Paul's day the most likely source of irreconcilable conflict would have been the issue of idol worship. Among pagan Corinthians, commerce, socializing, and family all involved worshipping idols. Followers of the one true God could not in good conscience participate in those rituals, which frequently put believers in an awkward position with family, friends, and associates. Those who were slaves faced an especially difficult dilemma.

Paul underlined his point with several rhetorical questions (2 Cor. 6:14–16):

- What do righteousness and wickedness have in common?
- What fellowship can light have with darkness?
- What harmony is there between Christ and Belial (Satan)?
- What does a believer have in common with an unbeliever?
- What agreement is there between the temple of God and idols?

The apostle concluded with a blended quotation from Leviticus, Jeremiah, and Ezekiel: "Therefore, 'Come out from them and be separate, says the Lord. Touch no unclean thing, and I will receive you.' And 'I will be a Father to you, and you will be my sons and daughters, says the Lord Almighty'" (2 Cor. 6:17–18).

Paul made clear in his earlier letter that he was not demanding a monastic withdrawal from the world, which he acknowledged would be impractical (1 Cor. 5:9–10). Rather, he forbade alliances that claimed a nonexistent spiritual unity (v. 11). In our day the idols have changed, but the conflicts that arise between followers of Jesus and those who bow to other gods remain.

Paul's warning should give us pause as we consider our modern-day political alliances. We need to distinguish cooperation on specific goals—what is sometimes called "co-belligerency"—from alliances that may tempt us to downplay important convictions. We face several probing questions:

1. In twenty-first-century America, does deep engagement in partisan political life, where the party platforms espouse commitments that Christians cannot support, involve us in an unequal yoke?

2. Should most Christians be political independents and cooperate with the parties without being co-opted by them? Is this practical for politicians who come from states or districts where one political party predominates?

3. Should Christians who engage deeply in politics be encouraged to establish or join a nonpartisan or bipartisan accountability group to keep themselves spiritually healthy?

4. Are advocacy alliances that bring together strange bedfellows acceptable?

The very term "bedfellows," with its allusion to a sexual relationship, should alert us to the dangers. Christians should tread very carefully here, cooperating on issues without being unequally yoked with groups that may be pulling in a different direction. We should prayerfully vote our consciences, not uncritically support a particular party.

DEALING WITH DETRACTORS

Balancing the warning against idolatrous alliances is the reassurance of God's sovereignty and mercy. In his letter to the Philippians, Paul took an expansive view of God's ability and willingness to work through a wide variety of persons and circumstances. Paul's imprisonment brought the gospel message to his captors and even to the whole palace guard. And his example inspired others:

Because of my chains, most of the brothers and sisters have become confident in the Lord and dare all the more to proclaim the gospel without fear.

It is true that some preach Christ out of envy and rivalry, but others out of goodwill. The latter do so out of love, knowing that I am put here for the defense of the gospel. The former preach Christ out of selfish ambition, not sincerely, supposing that they can stir up trouble for me while I am in chains. But what does it matter? The important thing is that in every way, whether from false motives or true, Christ is preached. And because of this I rejoice (Phil. 1:14–18).

Paul had healthy self-esteem, but he was not egotistical. When some of his competitors tried to steal his thunder, Paul did not become hooked in a battle for preeminence. He acknowledged that their motives were wrong, but he celebrated God's ability to bring good out of evil. As we see others in the church and in the Christian community whose approach is different from ours, and who may even be our critics, we can learn from Paul's patient faith that God will work things out. We can't always get fellow believers to see things our way. The reverse is also true. But we can pray for one another, treat one another with respect, and trust God's sovereignty regardless of who "wins."

A CALL TO CONVICTION AND COMPROMISE

A *conviction* is "a firmly held belief or opinion." Christians have convictions that grow out of our understanding of biblical teaching, our relationship with God, and our experience of learning as we follow Jesus Christ as members of his church and are led by the Holy Spirit. Our understanding is partial and finite, only a reflection of the truth that we will encounter when we see Jesus face-to-face (1 Cor. 13:12). But we are responsible to live by the light that God has given us and have the courage of our convictions.

Compromise is "a settlement of differences by mutual concessions."[3] This works well when two people both want the last piece of cake. They can agree to split it—with one person doing the cutting and the other person getting the first choice. But it doesn't work when the object of contention can't be divided, as in the story of King Solomon and the baby claimed by two mothers (1 Kings 3:16–28).

Yet, *compromise* is also an ambiguous word. It can mean "selling out," as when someone is compromised by a bribe or moral failure. That kind of compromise should be strictly avoided. At times when our core commitments are at stake, the saints and martyrs are our guides. When we are commanded to deny our faith or directly violate biblical principles, we need to say with Martin Luther, "My conscience is captive to the Word of God. I cannot and I will not recant anything."[4]

But many disagreements are over matters of judgment, not principle. We agree on basic goals, such as fighting poverty or giving our children a good education. There are many approaches to achieving these goals. Approaches can sometimes be combined, but if not, more than one approach may still succeed.

In a democracy, no side gets everything it wants. Democracy is a messy business of give and take, of shifting alliances, of 24/7 news cycles. The legislative process is often referred to as "sausage making." The result may be delicious, but you don't want to know what went into it. Purists are shocked, but the people's business—at least some of it—gets done.

Many times politicians aren't in a hurry to compromise because conflict over a hot-button issue can increase and solidify support. When the federal government briefly shut down in 2013, politicians set new fundraising records.[5] Why resolve the issue when both sides are using it for partisan advantage?

Win/win compromises are made more difficult by a cavalier approach to the truth in what passes for political debate. To make their point and garner your support, both sides often exaggerate their claims, present an extreme example as the norm, or invoke a parade of horribles. They commission "push polls," using carefully worded questions designed to prove that the public supports a particular view, while a competing poll proves the opposite. The public itself is alternately confused or bemused.

In this confusing and conflicted environment, how can we disagree politically without becoming disagreeable? Here are a few suggestions:

- *Listen carefully.* Understand the concerns and proposed solutions. Find out what is really important to those with whom you disagree.

- *Look for common ground.* Where do you agree, despite disagreement elsewhere?

- *Personalize the relationship, not the argument.* Disagree with a smile. Remember that your adversary today may be your ally tomorrow on another issue. And your loving engagement across differences may be the thing that brings others to Christ.

Chapter 17

WINNING AND LOSING

On Tuesday evening, November 7, 2000, Americans went to bed not knowing who had been elected as their next president. More than a month of recounts, court challenges, and nonstop press coverage followed, until the Supreme Court brought the whole process to an end on December 12 with a 5-4 vote in favor of George W. Bush. By a 537-vote margin out of nearly 6 million votes cast, Bush won Florida's 25 electoral votes and with them the presidency. Bush narrowly defeated Vice President Al Gore even though Gore's nationwide popular vote total exceeded Bush's by more than half a million votes.

While the 2000 presidential election was particularly dramatic, there is always a sharp contrast in mood at the winning and losing campaign headquarters. Unlike some systems that feature proportional representation, American elections are winner-take-all affairs.

Americans may have taken for granted that the Supreme Court's decision in *Bush v. Gore* would be accepted and that there would be another peaceful transfer of power from one political party to another despite the disputed outcome and a feeling on the part of some Gore supporters that the election had been "stolen." In many countries this peaceful transfer would not have been the case.

Watching news of the election returns from Sierra Leone, where I (Galen) was overseeing relief operations for World Relief, I marveled at the contrast. Sierra Leone, a war-torn West African country, was nine years into a violent power struggle. In 1991, with support from Liberia, rebels sought a change in government, not through ballots, but with bullets and butcher knives. As the fighting dragged on, with neither side able to defeat the other, gangs of youth high on drugs terrorized villagers, raping and murdering. A common practice was chopping off a person's arm or a leg or both. More than 50,000 Sierra Leoneans died in the eleven-year civil war, and more than a million were displaced from their homes before the rebels were finally defeated in 2002.[1] Sierra Leone has still not fully recovered from this national nightmare.

Even when they don't result in civil wars or rebellions, electoral campaigns are often hard-fought contests in which both sides vigorously attack the other. Those disinterested in politics still absorb some of the vitriol as they watch campaign commercial after campaign commercial and digest a barrage of blogs, emails, and online commentary. Campaign volunteers and supporters often feel deeply the agony of defeat or the ecstasy of victory. This raises challenges for both sides.

Those whose candidates are defeated may fear that the city/state/nation is on a path to destruction. Exaggerated predictions of doom often circulate via chain emails. If the election was close, there may be allegations of fraud or misconduct. The result is divisive rhetoric that can poison relationships at church, in the workplace, between neighbors, or even at home.

Supporters of the winning candidate may seek to press the advantage by pushing for actions that effectively punish the losers. They may have unrealistic expectations for the changes that the new candidate seeks to bring. When these changes don't immediately materialize, the winning voters may become disillusioned, even cynical.

Like elections, wars produce losers, though not always winners. The side that seems to have won often overreaches in ways that come back to undermine what was won. After World War I, the Allies imposed harsh conditions on the vanquished Germans, including unrealistic reparations.[2] The resulting suffering and bitterness created fertile ground for the rise of Adolf Hitler. In contrast, after World War II, the Marshall Plan helped our defeated enemies rebuild. Germany and Japan are now among our closest allies.

Americans can be thankful for our nearly two and a half centuries of democratic rule in which, with the major exceptions of the Revolutionary and Civil Wars, governmental transitions have taken place peacefully at the ballot box. Yet, we could do much better. Our nation would be more prosperous and peaceful if more of us were humble winners and gracious losers. As Christians, we are called to a higher standard.

THE BIBLE ON WINNING AND LOSING

The Bible opens on a high note and—spoiler alert—closes on an even higher note. God wins—and amazingly, invites us to his victory banquet. Confidence in God's sovereignty puts our personal and political wins and losses into perspective. We can rejoice when our candidates win, without placing our confidence in them. We can also accept our losses in elections, knowing that God works through them as well and can use them to bring about a greater victory.

For example, when Joseph was sold by his brothers into slavery, he seemed destined for a miserable life and an early death. But Joseph learned to depend on God's provision in the midst of great suffering and loss. In doing so, he allowed God to shape his character. God honored his faithfulness and raised him to a position of great responsibility in Egypt. Joseph was used by God to prevent widespread starvation in a famine.

Joseph's character and dependence on God, forged through

trials, enabled him to handle success and winning well. He forgave his brothers and chose to see God's hand at work even in
their treachery. He didn't sugarcoat their behavior, but reframed it.
"You intended to harm me, but God intended it for good" (Gen.
50:20). What if Joseph had instead taken revenge on his brothers
and killed them all? God's promises to Abraham would, humanly
speaking, have come to an end.

This story can help us whether we are political winners or losers. When our candidate loses, we can remember that God may
have purposes that are unknown to us. At some level, our political
opponents probably mean to do good through their political service. But even if they mean to do evil, God can still work his will.
This awareness should give us quiet confidence no matter who our
leaders are or what policies they pursue.

When our candidate wins, we should beware of vindictiveness.
Those who supported the other candidate probably meant well,
and they may have legitimate concerns that need to be taken into
account. We should encourage our leaders to look for opportunities
to cooperate with their political opponents in the national interest.

Winning in politics is a path to power. Power can be used for
good or evil. Jesus warned against using wealth and power for self-
serving purposes:

- The farmer who spent his time planning bigger barns for
  his surplus grain produced by his ground was called a fool
  for not being "rich toward God" (Luke 12:16–21).
- The rich man who ignored the beggar Lazarus at his gate
  found himself in hell, while Lazarus was with Abraham in
  heaven (Luke 16:19–31).
- The ungodly judge who delayed justice for the widow was
  eventually overcome by her persistence (Luke 18:1–8).

- The unmerciful servant who, having been forgiven a great debt, failed to forgive the much smaller debt of a fellow servant, thus turning a huge win into a tortured existence in debtors prison (Matt. 18:23–30).

- The murderous tenants who tried to steal their master's estate by killing his servants and even his son, rather than receive an undeserved inheritance, had their lives come to a "wretched end" (Matt. 21: 33–41).

- The goats in Matthew's judgment scene failed to care for the hungry, thirsty, homeless, naked, and imprisoned, and they were sent away to their eternal punishment (Matt. 25: 31–46).

Instead of focusing on self-centered "winning," Jesus invites us to "seek first his kingdom" in all things, including our politics (Matt. 6:33).

We should remember that human wins and losses are never permanent. If we take advantage of others when our side is in power, we shouldn't be surprised when the other side retaliates the next time it regains power. How the candidates and their supporters respond to winning, or losing, says a lot about their character.

HANDLING VICTORY IN POLITICS

Winning can be spiritually hazardous. Winners are tempted to take credit for their success, forgetting their dependence on God.

Winning in politics doesn't directly bring money, but it can bring fame and power. Moses warned the Israelites not to allow success to harden their hearts:

Be careful that you do not forget the LORD your God, failing to observe his commands, his laws and his decrees that I am giving you this day. Otherwise, when you eat and are satisfied, when you build fine houses and settle down, and when your herds and flocks grow large and your silver and gold increase and all you have is multiplied, then your heart will become proud and you will forget the LORD your God, who brought you out of Egypt, out of the land of slavery....

You may say to yourself, "My power and the strength of my hands have produced this wealth for me." But remember the LORD your God, for it is he who gives you the ability to produce wealth, and so confirms his covenant, which he swore to your forefathers, as it is today.

If you ever forget the LORD your God and follow other gods and worship and bow down to them, I testify against you today that you will surely be destroyed (Deut. 8:11–14, 17–19).

Moses knew that success often undermines future success by producing pride and idolatry. That way, he warned, is the path of destruction. His predictions sadly came true, again and again.

King David won impressive military victories and composed many of the Bible's psalms, but at some point he decided that the Ten Commandments no longer applied to him. He committed adultery and then murder to cover it up, with disastrous results for the nation (2 Sam. 11–12). David's son Solomon led the nation to unprecedented prosperity, but then used his power to accumulate a thousand wives and concubines, many from foreign countries. The wives brought their religions with them, and soon the nation fell into idolatry (1 Kings 10:23–11:13).

Four basic insights can be discerned from the biblical warnings and the lessons of history:

- *Victory is unstable.* Today's winners are often tomorrow's losers. Keep your trust in God, not your political party or leader. Don't fall into the traps of complacency or pride. "Pride goes before destruction, a haughty spirit before a fall" (Prov. 16:18).

185

- *Victory can be disappointing.* Candidates often promise more than they can deliver. Many present oversimplified analysis and gloss over obstacles. They imagine, or at least pretend, that solutions are easy and can be quickly achieved without shared sacrifice, if only the right policies are put in place.

  Have realistic expectations, and beware of being used. Evangelicals are a coveted constituency comprising about 25 percent of the population. Politicians seeking evangelical votes often appeal to a shared personal faith or commitment to certain values as the basis for support. But to get elected, candidates must build a coalition of multiple constituencies, not all of whom can be satisfied. It is important to have realistic expectations, and to be vigilant.

- *Governing is often harder than winning elections.* Diagnoses and solutions that seem obvious to the outsider prove to be more complex once the candidate is in office and gains fuller understanding of the complexity of issues. Vested interests come to light. Supporters who contributed and volunteered during the campaign expect to be rewarded. In order to please some constituents, others must be disappointed. That is the nature of governing, whether the governed are a family, church, or nation.

- *Wise winners work for reconciliation.* Supporters may press their leader for immediate results. In a situation of conflict, they may push for retribution against their political opponents. In too many countries this leads to violent repression, even murder, of opposition leaders. A more hopeful example comes from South Africa, where a Truth and Reconciliation Commission brought the offenses of the apartheid regime into the light, but also offered forgiveness and restoration to those who confessed. Winners who overreach risk creating a backlash that undermines the goals for which they worked so hard.

HANDLING POLITICAL DEFEAT

Losing graciously isn't easy, particularly when important issues are at stake. The security, prosperity, freedom, or morality of the nation may be threatened by the ill-considered policies of the new leader. Or so it seems.

Yet, just as the promises of a candidate often remain unfulfilled, so, too, the doom and gloom predicted if the other side wins often does not materialize. Leaders influence the direction of a society, but many factors are beyond their control.

In other words, if your candidate is not moving into the White House, it won't be the end of the world, and it does not help anything to grumble and complain.

Ultimately, Christians believe that God is in control of both the world we see and the unseen world that is beyond our experience. God's ways are not our ways. God is not limited to working through one political party, ideology, or approach. God raises up leaders—and he brings leaders down.

Does this mean that politics is a waste of time, that our actions don't make a difference? Far from it! (Just ask those 537 Florida voters.) As with every area of life, we are called by God to be partners with him, co-creators. As Saint Augustine is often quoted as saying, "Without God, we cannot. Without us, God will not." We are called to persist in doing good even in discouraging circumstances (Rom. 2:7; Gal. 6:9). Such circumstances are used by God to develop godly character in us, just as he did in Joseph.

Godly character does not include name-calling, insults, and personal attacks. Our Christian testimony is not enhanced when we resort to slander and mudslinging. Rather than withdrawing or throwing up our hands in despair, we can be the loyal opposition. Start by praying for our leaders, even—perhaps especially—when you disagree with them. Look for things to commend, areas of agreement. Be positive when you can, praising what is praiseworthy.

When you must differ, disagree over issues thoughtfully and without exaggeration. Don't personalize; don't attack the person; don't impugn motives. Remember that your opponents also bear God's image. Only God can see the heart. We see behaviors, but the source of those behaviors may be known only to God. Instead of just criticizing, suggest alternatives. Look for opposition leaders who do the same.

In Hebrews 12:15 we are warned to "See to it that no one falls short of the grace of God and that no bitter root grows up to cause trouble and defile many." James identifies bitter envy and selfish ambition as the breeding grounds for "disorder and every evil practice" (James 3:16). Maintaining a discipline of gratitude, on the other hand, protects our hope.

Disappointment and disillusionment with politics and government can also lead to cynicism, the inability to trust in the sincerity of others. Cynicism abandons healthy discernment in favor of prejudice and despair. Like bitterness, cynicism is toxic to a healthy political process. It can lead to sweeping calls to "throw the bums out." This attitude disrespects the work God is doing through our leaders.

We should not become discouraged when our political goals are not immediately achieved. Losing can teach us to wait on the Lord who hears our cries and comforts us in times of disappointment and uncertainty.

JESUS IS LORD

The ultimate political statement is "Jesus is Lord." Quoting an ancient hymn, Paul challenged believers to have the same attitude as Jesus Christ:

> *Who, being in very nature God,*
> *did not consider equality with God*
> *something to be used to his own advantage;*
> *rather, he made himself nothing*
> *by taking the very nature of a servant,*
> *being made in human likeness.*
> *And being found in appearance as a man,*
> *he humbled himself*
> *by becoming obedient to death—*
> *even death on a cross!*
> *Therefore God exalted him to the highest place*
> *and gave him the name that is above every name,*
> *that at the name of Jesus every knee should bow,*
> *in heaven and on earth and under the earth,*
> *and every tongue acknowledge that Jesus Christ is Lord,*
> *to the glory of God the Father* (Phil. 2:6–11).

Jesus teaches us that the Father can be trusted even on the cross. Whether we win or lose at the polls, we know that Jesus has been given all authority in heaven and on earth and that he promises to be with us always (Matt. 28:18, 20). Confident of God's gracious presence and provision, we can be his witnesses even in our voting and our politics.

Chapter 18

A CALL FOR CIVILITY

In January 2009 the Civility Project was launched by Republican Mark DeMoss and Democrat Lanny Davis. They wrote letters to all 100 U.S. senators, 435 members of the U.S. House of Representatives, and 50 state governors. They were asked to sign the following pledge: *I will be civil in my public discourse and behavior. I will be respectful of others whether or not I agree with them. I will stand against incivility when I see it.* Out of the 585 asked to sign, only three said, "Yes."[1]

Though it is tempting to join the incivility of the current political world, we are called to the higher purposeful civility of Christian witness.

When Rome burned in July of AD 64, the citizens of the city blamed Emperor Nero. The emperor made a political decision to turn the blame away from himself and lay it on Christians, who were then tortured and executed. Amazingly, many of those persecuted Christians lived out their faith in ways that persuaded some of their executioners to become believers because they saw the way Christians died.

Eventually Christian behavior led to a majority of the population becoming Christians and the empire itself being declared Christian. They heeded the advice of the apostle Peter, who wrote in AD 67, "Live such good lives among the pagans that, though they accuse you of doing wrong, they may see your good deeds and glorify God" (1 Peter 2:12). One definition of *glorify* is to

190

make someone "look good." Those early followers of Jesus were challenged to make God look good to the pagans who were persecuting them.

In too many parts of today's world, Christians are suffering at a level paralleling Roman times—persecution, beheadings, and crucifixions. In America we have been safe and secure in a democracy that we share with over 300 million other people. Our Christian approach should be civility in our words and actions toward pagans and fellow Christians, with those who agree and disagree, with friends and enemies alike. "Whether you eat or drink or whatever you do, do it all for the glory of God" (1 Cor. 10:31).

CIVILITY VS. INCIVILITY

Incivility is old. Records of animosity and arrogance go back as far as written human history. And there was no shortage in early chapters of American history. Statements by John Adams and Thomas Jefferson about each other two centuries ago are so racially offensive that no one should be able to muster the courage to read them out loud.

Susan Herbst, a scholar and author, acknowledges that incivility is pretty bad today, but that the nation's low point was in the 1850s leading up to the Civil War. She says, "The country was so incredibly divided. Fist fights broke out on the floor of Congress. We're certainly not at that low point now, but it's absolutely one of the worst times we've had."[2]

What is different today is the amplification of our incivility by the Internet and other media. Messages can be sent by anyone. Instantly. Offensive statements can reach millions in nanoseconds.

Today's differences are real. We have profound disagreements on social, economic, religious, and political issues. No one should be surprised that there are real differences among our hundreds of millions. But differences and diversity are no excuses for rudeness, unkindness, name-calling, and other un-Christian words and actions.

While many try to simplify today's issues and offer easy solutions, the issues are usually very complex. Whether we are talking about health care, budget deficits, or nuclear weapons, we can list thousands of variables. Few of us can grasp the complexity. We want simple explanations. Yet, simple explanations may be invalid if not disingenuous. Take reducing poverty, for example. Everyone agrees that we should try to do this, but it's not as simple as handing out money directly or letting it trickle down. Real solutions cannot be reduced to sound bites, and demonizing the opposition does little to help the poor.

Are we supposed to compromise or abandon our sincere convictions in order to be nice? Of course not. It's good to have convictions. We should beware of tolerating wrong in the quest to be civil. University of Chicago historian Martin Marty says that "one of the real problems in modern life is that the people who are good at being civil often lack strong convictions and people who have strong convictions often lack civility."[3]

BIBLICAL CIVILITY

It is easy to be uncivil and impolite, whether driving down the interstate or debating public policy. It can feel good to win a verbal debate with a derogatory put-down. Negative ads can be very effective. Mean-spirited attacks in blogs, speeches, and social media may give a sense of victory over enemies. Anonymous comments on Internet sites or social media are often vicious; words are posted that are intended to harm by attackers who are empowered by the freedom and anonymity of a keyboard and a computer. In many ways incivility is the easy option. Civility is hard work. Civility is a choice.

Richard Mouw, in his book *Uncommon Decency*, defines *civility* as "public politeness."[4] Expressions of politeness vary in different cultures, but most of us know what it looks and sounds like in America. Politeness shows respect for others, avoids offensive words, tells the truth, listens to another's point of view, and shows kind thoughtfulness. None of this requires us to abandon our principles, compromise our values, or surrender the truth. In its simplest expression, civility brings Jesus' Golden Rule into politics by doing "to others as you would have them do to you" (Luke 6:31).

Old Testament wisdom recognized the practical value of civility by teaching that "A gentle answer turns away wrath, but a harsh word stirs up anger" (Prov. 15:1). This advice came from King Solomon, who was a career politician. In the New Testament, Paul speaks as a preacher—not a politician—when he says that "the Lord's servant must not be quarrelsome but must be kind to everyone" (2 Tim. 2:24). To argue is to give reasons for or against something.

To quarrel is to have a violent disagreement that breaks off friendly relations.

PRACTICING CHRISTIAN CIVILITY

Faith begins with what we believe, but it doesn't end with a creed or list of doctrines. Faith includes what we do and how we live.

The expectations of faithful Christian living taught in James 2 apply to Christian civility in politics:

- "If you really keep the royal law found in Scripture, 'Love your neighbor as yourself,' you are doing right" (v. 8).

- "Speak and act as those who are going to be judged by the law that gives freedom, because judgment without mercy will be shown to anyone who has not been merciful. Mercy triumphs over judgment" (vv. 12–13).

In order to practice Christian civility we may need some personal repentance, mouth cleaning, and heart change. Ephesians 4:31 comes directly to the point: "Get rid of all bitterness, rage and anger, brawling and slander, along with every form of malice." Some should retract past statements and ask forgiveness from those they mistreated. Let's ask ourselves, "Have I spoken disrespectfully about a current or past president? Have I forwarded an email joke that belittles a politician? Have I repeated things about a politician that I suspected were untrue, but said them anyway because I knew it would get the response I wanted?" Not easy, but powerfully good.

When we love our neighbors and speak and act with mercy, we practice Christian civility. Can one Christian make a difference? Probably not. We may not unilaterally depolarize politics or eliminate incivility. But we can make a difference together. Along with our pastors, small group members, and a few more friends, we can start a movement. Movements often begin with individuals. Besides, none of us is exempt from the words of Paul: "If it is possible, as far as it depends on you, live at peace with everyone" (Rom. 12:18).

Civility certainly includes direct conversations with anyone about politics. Civility is also required in the words we speak about those who are not present, the sentences we write on a computer screen, the jokes we tell, the cartoons we draw, and the attitudes we have. As Christians, we can set an example for others to experience and follow.

Sadly, some Christians adopt the tactics of unbelievers. Critics claim that religious people are the least civil of society. Some religious leaders are known for personal attacks, describing those who differ as "left leaning," "right wing," "extremely liberal," or "extremely conservative" even when such descriptions are inaccurate and unfair. The specific terms are less important than the lack of love in their incivility.

What should we do if we are unfairly labeled or criticized or see it happening to others? Respond with politeness. Don't repeat uncivil words. Avoid forwarding or repeating the incivility of others even if we agree with that person's politics. Cancel subscriptions to publications that major in incivility. Don't vote for candidates who are uncivil, and write to tell them why. Don't contribute money in response to fundraising letters that attack others and distort the truth. In other words, break the cycle of un-Christian incivility.

KINGDOM COME

Hostile words, name-calling, shouting, hatred, half-truths, untruthful exaggerations, and other acts of incivility usually don't persuade someone to change and agree. All they do is deepen the divide between people who already disagree and don't like each other.

The practice of Christian civility brings the fruit of the Spirit into the public square: "love, joy, peace, forbearance, kindness, goodness, faithfulness, gentleness and self-control" (Gal. 5:22–23). We please God, display the love of Jesus, and bless our nation all at the same time.

Christians around the world—citizens of every nation, speaking different languages, with diverse politics—pray the same prayer in church services and personal worship. The Lord's Prayer that Jesus taught us to pray is the centerpiece of our politics:

> *"Our Father in heaven,*
> *hallowed be your name,*
> *your kingdom come,*
> *your will be done,*
>   *on earth as it is in heaven"* (Matt. 6:9–10).

May our politics be Christlike and civil as we live out the values of the kingdom of heaven here on earth.

ENDNOTES

CHAPTER 1: WHY WE WROTE THIS BOOK

1. "America's Changing Religious Landscape," Pew Research Center (May 12, 2015), 2, http://www.pewforum.org/2015/05/12/americas-changing-religious-landscape/.
2. "A Deep Dive into Party Affiliation," Pew Research Center (April 7, 2015), 3, http://www.people-press.org/2015/04/07/a-deep-dive-into-party-affiliation/.
3. "Voter Turnout," The Center for Voting and Democracy, http://www.fairvote.org/research-and-analysis/voter-turnout/ (accessed July 4, 2015).
4. See www.nae.net.

CHAPTER 2: HOW TO VOTE

1. Mark N. Franklin, *Voter Turnout and the Dynamics of Electoral Competition in Established Democracies Since 1945* (New York: Cambridge University Press, 2004), 11, Table I.I.

CHAPTER 4: CHRISTIANS AND EVANGELICALS

1. Leith Anderson, "Science and Faith—Connecting Communities," Dialogue on Science, Ethics, and Religion at the Perceptions Conference of the American Association for the Advancement of Science (Washington, DC, March 13, 2015), http://www.aaas.org/news/watch-perceptions-conference.

2. The NAE has adopted a recommended research definition of *evangelical*, which is available here: http://nae.net/evangelical -beliefs-research-definition/.

3. The "Bebbington Quadrilateral" in his book *Evangelicalism in Modern Britain: A History from the 1730s to the 1980s* (London: Unwin Hyman, 1989). David Bebbington covers these four convictions under the terms Conversionism, Activism, Biblicism, and Crucicentrism.

4. See http://www.worldea.org/whoweare/introduction.

CHAPTER 5: CHRISTIANS AND POLITICS: DO THEY MIX?

1. Immigrant Archive Project, https://www.youtube.com/watch? v=Za4ZZN0SekE (accessed July 8, 2015). Only one of fifteen native-born Americans interviewed correctly answered six of ten questions and thus passed the citizenship test.

2. Then-U.S. Senator Mark Hatfield, in his 1976 book *Between a Rock and a Hard Place* (Dallas: Word Books, 1976), argues that we must keep both images in tension.

3. See, for instance, in the book of Exodus the Ten Commandments (20:1–17), economic laws (chaps. 21–22), political laws (23:1–9, 20–33), and religious laws (23:10–19; chaps. 25–31; 35:1–39:30).

4. See also 1 Peter 2:13–15.

5. See http://kingwatch.co.nz/Prophetic_Ministry/prophet_to_ nation.htm (accessed July 6, 2015).

6. *Wisconsin v. Yoder*, 406 U.S. 205 (1972). The Court ruled that Wisconsin's compulsory school attendance law for all children under age sixteen violated the First Amendment, imposing on Amish children values that were "in sharp conflict with the fundamental mode of life mandated by the Amish religion."

7. An influential book he wrote was *The Uneasy Conscience of Modern Fundamentalism* (Grand Rapids: Eerdmans, 1947).

8. Some media outlets erroneously treat "evangelical" and

"Religious Right" as synonyms. Evangelicals, however, define themselves on theological, not political, grounds.

9. Available at www.nae.net.

10. See http://www.gallup.com/poll/180440/new-record-political -independents.aspx (accessed July 10, 2015).

11. National Association of Evangelicals, "For the Health of the Nation: An Evangelical Call to Civic Responsibility," 9, available at www.nae.net.

12. See http://www.searchquotes.com/Winston_Churchill/ Government/quotes/ (accessed September 30, 2015).

13. Information about the Offering of Letters concept can be found at www.bread.org.

14. While pastors arguably have a First Amendment right to express political opinions and candidate preferences in their sermons, this is almost always a bad idea and should be avoided.

15. See http://www.washingtoninst.org/235/the-culture-is-upstream -from-politics/ (accessed July 4, 2015).

16. See http://www.scotusblog.com/case-files/cases/shelby-county-v -holder/.

17. See http://mentalfloss.com/article/59873/10-elections-decided -one-vote-or-less (accessed July 3, 2015).

18. See http://penews.org/Article/Statement-Regarding-the-Supreme -Court-s-Same-Sex-Marriage-Decision/#sthash.JKDPHvOa.dpuf (accessed June 29, 2015).

CHAPTER 6: PRINCIPLES AND PRIORITIES

1. "Circumcision remains legal in Germany," http://www.dw.com/ en/circumcision-remains-legal-in-germany/a-16399336.

2. History has sad stories of dictators and philosophies committed to the notion that the end always justifies the means. This idea has been used to justify genocide and other atrocities with the claim that future generations will be better off. Christian

commitment to the common good includes immediate good as well as future good and requires ethical actions for everyone.

3. See http://www.tipsonlifeandlove.com/your-money-and-career/there-can-only-be-one-no-1-the-best-kept-secret-about-priorities.

CHAPTER 7: WHERE MOST EVANGELICALS AGREE MOST OF THE TIME

1. Linton Weeks, "A Nation Divided: Can We Agree on Anything?" on National Public Radio (February 28, 2012), http://www.npr.org/2012/02/28/147338798/disagreeable-america-can-t-we-all-just-get-along.

2. The examples of unfulfilled predictions from political analysts, religious writers, and others are easy to research. No examples are cited here, because the point is not to draw attention to failed prophecies, but to emphasize that we must be careful about predictions.

3. Article III, Section 3 of the U.S. Constitution says,

"Treason against the United States, shall consist only in levying war against them, or in adhering to their enemies, giving them aid and comfort. No person shall be convicted of treason unless on the testimony of two witnesses to the same overt act, or on confession in open court.

"The Congress shall have power to declare the punishment of treason, but no attainder of treason shall work corruption of blood, or forfeiture except during the life of the person attainted."

There is debate over how many, if any, have ever been executed by the federal government for treason. In 1953 Julius and Ethel Rosenberg were executed for espionage. Others were executed by states for treason in early U.S. history. Even if scholars claim that there have been federal executions for treason, the list is extremely short.

4. For a discussion of the issue see the NAE's resolution on capital punishment, available at http://nae.net/capital-punishment-2/.

5. In Psalm 139:13–15, King David said that he was "knit ... together in my mother's womb." Exodus 21:22–24 specifies criminal punishment for someone who causes harm to an unborn child even when it is the secondary consequence of a fight.

6. Lydia Saad, "Americans Choose 'Pro-Choice' for First Time in Seven Years," Gallup (May 29, 2015), http://www.gallup.com/poll/ 183434/americans-choose-pro-choice-first-time-seven-years.aspx.

7. The Religious Freedom Restoration Act (RFRA) establishes a balancing test, allowing government to enforce laws that substantially burden a sincere religious belief only when using the least restrictive means to achieve a compelling government interest. See a helpful infographic at http://1stamendmentpartnership.s3 .amazonaws.com/wp-content/uploads/FAM101-How-RFRA -Works-Infographic-R5.png (accessed October 19, 2015).

CHAPTER 8: WHAT TO DO ABOUT POVERTY

1. "Leeching nutrients. Stealing lives," World Vision email from Rich Stearns, president (July 2, 2015).

2. Shankar Vedantam, "Why Your Brain Wants to Help One Child in Need—But Not Millions," on National Public Radio (November 5, 2014), http://www.npr.org/sections/ goatsandsoda/2014/11/05/361433850/why-your-brain-wants-to -help-one-child-in-need-but-not-millions.

3. "Poor Children," Humanium, http://www.humanium.org/en/ poor-children/ (September 26, 2011).

4. See http://www.wateraid.org/us/the-water-story/the-crisis/ statistics?id=annual,G,GGL,GAW&gclid=CP-YiJ_678YCFRCC aQodQF8Nqg.

5. "Overview," World Bank (updated April 6, 2015), http://www .worldbank.org/en/topic/poverty/overview.

6. "Poverty" definition, BusinessDictionary.com. at http://www
   .businessdictionary.com/definition/poverty.html#ixzz3g76TjCk9.
7. "Overview," World Bank (updated April 6, 2015), http://www
   .worldbank.org/en/topic/poverty/overview.
8. "Income, Poverty and Health Insurance Coverage in the United
   States: 2013," U.S. Census Bureau, Release Number: CB14
   -169 (September 16, 2014), http://www.census.gov/newsroom/
   press-releases/2014/cb14-169.html. For a treatment of absolute
   poverty in America, see Kathryn J. Eden and H. Luke Shaefer,
   $2.00 a Day: Living on Almost Nothing in America (New York:
   Houghton Mifflin, Harcourt Publishing Company, 2015).
9. See http://www.pewtrusts.org/en/research-and-analysis/blogs/
   stateline/2015/3/19/the-shrinking-middle-class-mapped-state-by
   -state (accessed September 4, 2015).
10. See http://www.census.gov/housing/census/publications/who
    -can-afford.pdf (accessed September 4, 2015).
11. In his academically researched book with dozens of interesting
    stories, Robert Putnam of Harvard University has discovered
    that there is a growing caste system in our nation that
    increasingly keeps the poor poor and makes the rich richer.
    His focus is on children, so he titled his bestseller *Our Kids*. He
    explains how upper-class families nurture their children, help
    schools to provide excellent education, pay for extracurricular
    clubs and sports, and help them find jobs and get into college.
    These advantages position their children to succeed over children
    who are disadvantaged. The advantages are passed from one
    generation to the next. See Robert D. Putnam, *Our Kids: The
    American Dream in Crisis* (New York: Simon & Schuster, 2015).
12. Marisol Bello, "As seniors climb from poverty, young fall in,"
    USA Today (updated February 16, 2012), http://usatoday30.
    usatoday.com/news/nation/story/2012-02-16/child-senior
    -poverty/53107636/1.

202

13. "Goals, Targets and Indicators," MillenniumProject, http://www
.unmillenniumproject.org/goals/gti.htm#goal1.

14. "Overview," World Bank (updated April 6, 2015), http://www
.worldbank.org/en/topic/poverty/overview.

15. "Towards the End of Poverty," *The Economist* (June 1,
2013), http://www.economist.com/news/leaders/21578665-
nearly-1-billion-people-have-been-taken-out
-extreme-poverty-20-years-world-should-aim.

16. Bello, "As seniors climb from poverty, young fall in."

17. The Poverty and Justice Bible, American Bible Society, http://
www.bibles.com/cev-poverty-justice-bible-american-bible-society
-edition.html.

18. See http://www.compassion.com/poverty/what-the-bible-says
-about-poverty.htm.

19. An alternative is to use the search feature on the website Bible
Gateway, https://www.biblegateway.com/.

20. See Isaiah 61:1.

21. His first inaugural address as governor of California (January 5,
1967), http://governors.library.ca.gov/addresses/33-Reagan01.html.

22. John R. Coyne Jr., The Washington Times (July 15, 2015):
book review of The Conservative Heart: How to Build a Fairer,
Happier, and More Prosperous America by Arthur C. Brooks
(New York: Broadside Books, 2015).

23. Go to salvationarmyusa.org and enter a ZIP code to make a local
connection.

24. See https://www.youtube.com/watch?v=R9kv_v95mrg.

CHAPTER 9: A NATION OF MINORITIES

1. Russell Thornton, American Indian Holocaust and Survival:
A Population History Since 1492 (Norman: University of
Oklahoma Press, 1990), 15–41.

2. "CT1970p2-13: Colonial and Pre-Federal Statistics," U.S. Census Bureau (2004), 1168 (retrieved September 7, 2015).

3. Chinese "Exclusion Act" of 1882, Library of Congress, http://www.loc.gov/teachers/classroommaterials/presentationsand activities/presentations/immigration/chinese6.html (accessed September 7, 2015).

4. William H. Frey, "New Projections Point to a Majority Minority Nation in 2044," in The Avenue of the Brookings Institution (December 12, 2014), http://www.brookings.edu/blogs/the -avenue/posts/2014/12/12-majority-minority-nation-2044-frey.

5. Tanvi Misra, "Where Minority Populations Have Become the Majority," based on Pew Research Center projections from the U.S. Census Bureau 2013 population estimates, The Atlantic CITYLAB (April 9, 2015), http://www.brookings.edu/blogs/the -avenue/posts/2014/12/12-majority-minority-nation-2044-frey.

6. Frey, "New Projections Point to a Majority Minority Nation in 2044."

7. Luis Carlos Lopez, "Minorities Will Become the Majority in the U.S. by 2043," Huffington Post (March 25, 2013), http://www.huffingtonpost.com/2013/03/25/minorities-will-become -th_n_2948188.html.

8. Noor Wazwaz, "It's Official: The U.S. Is Becoming a Minority-Majority Nation," US News and World Report (July 6, 2015), http://www.usnews.com/news/articles/2015/07/06/its-official-the -us-is-becoming-a-minority-majority-nation.

9. Sean Reardon, "The Widening Achievement Gap Between the Rich and the Poor: New Evidence and Possible Explanations," in Whither Opportunity? Rising Inequality, Schools and Children's Life Chances, eds. Greg J. Duncan and Richard M. Murnane (New York: Russell Sage Foundation, 2011), cited in Robert D. Putnam, Our Kids: The American Dream in Crisis (New York: Simon & Schuster, 2015), 161f.

10. Wazwaz, "It's Official: The U.S. Is Becoming a Minority-Majority Nation."
11. David Brooks, "A Nation of Mutts," The New York Times (June 27, 2013), http://www.nytimes.com/2013/06/28/opinion/brooks -a-nation-of-mutts.html?_r=0.
12. The concept and issues related to racialization in America are addressed by Michael O. Emerson and Christian Smith, *Divided by Faith: Evangelical Religion and the Problem of Race in America* (New York: Oxford University Press, 2000).

CHAPTER 10: RECONNECTING SEX, MARRIAGE, FAMILY, AND CHILDREN

1. Cited by Rose M. and Renee Ellis Kreider, "Living Arrangements of Children: 2009," in *Current Population Reports*, P70-126, U.S. Census Bureau (2011), 8.
2. Ibid., 10. Approximately 42 million out of 74.1 million children, or 56.7 percent, lived with their biological married parents at the time of the Census Bureau interview. For African Americans it was 2.9 million out of 16.3 million children.
3. The stay-at-home parent is often but not always the mother. However, fathers can also perform well and experience satisfaction in full-time care-giving roles. See Noelle Chelsey, "Stay-at-Home Fathers and Breadwinning Mothers: Gender, Couple Dynamics and Social Change," *Gender and Society* 25, no. 5: 642–64 (October 2011).
4. For a discussion of sex in God's plan, see "Theology of Sex," available from the National Association of Evangelicals at www .nae.net.
5. See also Psalm 51.
6. See Ephesians 5:21–24.
7. As the story of the adulterous woman brought to Jesus illustrates,

women often bear the brunt of selective prosecution. See John 7:53–8:11.

8. Amnesty International, "Women in Afghanistan: The Back Story" (October 25, 2013), available at http://www.amnesty.org .uk/womens-rights-afghanistan-history#.VZ3uv_m6d1s (accessed July 8, 2015).

9. Mary Eberstadt and Mary Anne Layden, The Social Costs of Pornography: A Statement of Findings and Recommendations (Princeton, NJ: The Witherspoon Institute, 2010).

10. See www.endsexualexploitation.org.

11. A 2010 NAE survey reported that 90% of evangelical leaders surveyed approve of the use of artificial means of contraception. Survey results are available at http://nae.net/evangelical-leaders -are-ok-with-contraception/.

12. See http://www.scotusblog.com/case-files/cases/sebelius-v-hobby -lobby-stores-inc/ (accessed September 4, 2015).

13. For a thoughtful discussion of what could be done to help both mothers and the unborn, see Charles Camosy, *Beyond the Abortion Wars: A Way Forward for a New Generation* (Grand Rapids: Eerdmans, 2015).

14. See http://www.scotusblog.com/case-files/cases/obergefell-v -hodges/ (accessed July 6, 2015).

15. See Michael Reagan, *Twice Adopted* (Nashville: Broadman & Holman, 2004), 44.

16. Robert Putnam, *Our Kids: The American Dream in Crisis* (New York: Simon & Schuster, 2015), 248. "The best recent evidence is that on average the highest-quality child care, especially in the early years, comes from a child's own parents."

17. Ibid., 109ff.

18. See the NAE resolution "Child Care and the Federal Government," available at http://nae.net/child-care-and-the- federal-government-1989/.

19. Putnam, *Our Kids*, 109ff.

20. Putnam, citing Claudia Goldin and Lawrence Katz, calls the development of free secondary education in the United States "the seminal force behind both economic growth and socioeconomic equality in America during the twentieth century" (*Our Kids*, 160).

CHAPTER 11: WHAT WOULD THE STATUE OF LIBERTY SAY TODAY?

1. See http://www.statista.com/statistics/254218/number-of-visitors -to-the-statue-of-liberty-in-the-us/.
2. "Statue of Liberty," https://en.wikipedia.org/wiki/Statue_of_ Liberty.
3. "Immigration," http://www.globalissues.org/article/537/ immigration (updated May 26, 2008).
4. For a good summary of our immigration system, its problems, and some proposed solutions from an evangelical perspective, see Matthew Soerens and Jenny Hwang, *Welcoming the Stranger: Justice, Compassion and Truth in the Immigration Debate* (Downers Grove, IL: InterVarsity Press, 2009).
5. "Modes of Entry for the Unauthorized Migrant Population," Pew Hispanic Center (May 22, 2006), http://pewhispanic.org/files/ factsheets/19.pdf (accessed July 23, 2015).
6. "Real-Time Insight into the Market for Entry-Level STEM Jobs" (February 2014), available at http://burning-glass.com/research/ stem/ (accessed September 8, 2015).
7. For more on the economic impact of immigrants, see Galen Carey, "Immigration and the Economy: Beyond the Zero Sum Game," in the *Review of Faith and International Affairs* 9, no. 1 (Spring 2010).
8. See http://www.lifewayresearch.com/2015/03/11/evangelicals -say-it-is-time-for-congress-to-tackle-immigration/ (accessed July 23, 2015).

9. See also Leviticus 19:34.

10. See http://www.openbible.info/topics/immigration.

11. For a good survey of the Bible on immigration, see M. Daniel Carroll R., Christians at the Border: Immigration, the Church and the Bible (Grand Rapids: Baker Academic, 2008).

12. The explanation of biblical foundations, national realities, and call to action are at NAE.net/immigration.

13. See http://www.nytimes.com/roomfordebate/2012/12/09/understanding-immigration-reform/comprehensive-immigration-reform-means-no-stop-gap-solutions.

CHAPTER 12: WHO PAYS THE BILLS?

1. In 1992, 77% of upper-income tax payers agreed that they paid too little. In 2011 that number had declined to 59%, still the majority view. "American Public Opinion on Economic Inequality, Taxes and Mobility: 1990–2011," in *Public Opinion Quarterly* (Illinois Wesleyan University, October 2012), http://poq.oxfordjournals.org/content/early/2012/09/12/poq.nfs039.short?rss=1 and http://journalistsresource.org/studies/economics/inequality/american-us-public-opinion-economic-inequality-taxes-mobility (accessed July 11, 2015).

2. See http://www.pewtrusts.org/en/research-and-analysis/issue-briefs/2015/07/the-state-pensions-funding-gap-challenges-persist (accessed September 4, 2015).

3. See the discussion in chapter 5.

4. For contribution totals in recent years, see https://www.treasurydirect.gov/govt/reports/pd/gift/gift.htm (accessed July 14, 2015). Calculation based on approximate total federal spending of $3.5 trillion per year. See http://www.taxpolicycenter.org/taxfacts/displayafact.cfm?Docid=200 (accessed July 14, 2015).

5. See http://www.census.gov/library/publications/2014/demo/p60-249.html (accessed July 14, 2015).

6. See http://hirr.hartsem.edu/research/fastfacts/fast_facts.html #numcong (accessed July 14, 2015).

7. Documented in http://hirr.hartsem.edu/research/fastfacts/fast_facts.html#numcong (accessed July 14, 2015).

8. In 2014 the Supplemental Nutrition Assistance Program (SNAP) provided a monthly benefit of $125.35 to 46,536,000 low-income Americans for a total food cost of $70 billion (excluding $4.2 billion to administer the program). See www.fns.usda.gov/sites/default/files/pd/SNAPsummary.pdf (accessed July 14, 2015).

9. See, for example, 2 Kings 18:13–16.

10. See, for example, 2 Samuel 8:1–15.

11. The half-shekel was the equivalent to two drachma, or two days' wages. See Craig S. Keener, *The IVP Bible Background Commentary* (Downers Grove, IL: InterVarsity Press, 1976).

12. Richard Bauckham, *The Bible in Politics: How to Read the Bible Politically* (Louisville: Westminster/John Knox Press, 1989), 75.

13. In Roman Catholic social teaching, this principle is known as subsidiarity.

14. Federal income taxes reached a high of 94% at the end of World War II. See http://taxfoundation.org/article/us-federal-individual-income-tax-rates-history-1913-2013-nominal-and-inflation-adjusted-brackets (accessed July 14, 2015).

CHAPTER 13: JUSTICE AND JAILS

1. Billy Moore's testimony is told in his book, *I Shall Not Die: Seventy-two Hours on Death Watch* (Bloomington, IN: AuthorHouse, 2005).

2. See Robert Rotberg, "Failed States in a World of Terror," in *Foreign Affairs* (July/August 2002), published by the Council on Foreign Relations.

3. E. De Pauw et al., "Behavioral effects of fixed speed cameras on motorways: Overall improved speed compliance or kangaroo

jumps?" in *Accident Analysis and Prevention* (December 2014), 73:132–40. The study found that drivers did slow down for the cameras, but not before and after.

4. Federal Bureau of Investigation, Crime in the United States by Volume and Rate per 100,000 Inhabitants, 1994–2013, available at https://www.fbi.gov/about-us/cjis/ucr/crime-in-the-u.s/2013/crime-in-the-u.s.-2013/tables/1tabledatadecoverviewpdf/table_1_crime_in_the_united_states_by_volume_and_rate_per_100000_inhabitants_1994-2013.xls (accessed July 15, 2015).d Rate per 100,000 Inhabitants, 1994–2013

5. "DeRoche: Shared Values Are How to Structurally Change Washington" in *Roll Call* (May 28, 2013), available at http://www.rollcall.com/news/deroche_shared_values_are_how_to_structurally_change_washington-223350-1.html (accessed August 14, 2015).

6. National Association of Evangelicals, Sentencing Reform 1983, available at http://nae.net/sentencing-reform/.

7. Fred Osher et al., "Adults with Behavioral Health Needs Under Correctional Supervision: A Shared Framework for Reducing Recidivism and Promoting Recovery," Council of State Governments Justice Center, 2012, available at www.csgjusticecenter.org/wp-content/uploads/2013/05/9-24-12_Behavioral-Health-Framework-final.pdf (accessed July 13, 2015).

8. For an in-depth study, see Jennifer E. Walsh, *Three Strikes Laws* (Santa Barbara: Greenwood Publishing, 2007).

9. See the accounts in Matthew 27, Mark 15, Luke 23, and John 19.

10. See also the story of Zacchaeus, another reformed tax collector, in Luke 19:1–10.

11. See the NAE's 1997 resolution "The Church's Responsibility to Prisoners," available at www.nae.net/prisoners.

12. See Michelle Alexander, *The New Jim Crow: Mass Incarceration in the Age of Colorblindness* (New York: The New Press, 2010), for a detailed analysis of the role racial bias plays in criminal justice.

13. See George Will's column, "When Government is the Looter," in *The Washington Post* (May 18, 2012), available at http://www.washingtonpost.com/opinions/when-government-is-the-looter/2012/05/18/gIQAUIKVZU_story.html (accessed July 15, 2015).

14. See the NAE's letter and statement to Congress, "Limit the Use of Solitary Confinement in Prisons and Jails" (February 25, 2014), available at http://nae.net/limit-the-use-of-solitary-confinement-in-prisons-and-jails/ (accessed July 15, 2015).

15. See the NAE's statement on "Unjust Prison Phone Rates" (August 8, 2013), available at http://nae.net/unjust-prison-phone-rates/ (accessed July 15, 2015).

16. Grant Duwe and Byron R. Johnson, "Estimating the Benefits of a Faith-Based Correctional Program," in the *International Journal of Criminology and Sociology* (2013), 2: 227–39.

CHAPTER 14: JOHN 3:16 AND FOREIGN POLICY

1. See http://www.cdc.gov/vhf/ebola/outbreaks/2014-west-africa/qa-mmwr-estimating-future-cases.html (accessed July 21, 2015).

2. *Time* (December 10, 2014), available at www.time.com/time-person-of-the-year-ebola-doctors (accessed July 18, 2015).

3. The Africa Inland Mission, for example, began its work in Africa in 1895 and soon established a network of clinics, leprosariums, and basic hospitals. See www.aimint.org/usa/about/our-heritage (accessed July 18, 2015).

4. See www.nytimes.com/2015/03/29/opinion/sunday/nicholas-kristof-a-little-respect-for-dr-foster.html (accessed July 19, 2015).

5. R. J. Priest, "Introduction to Theme Issue on Short-Term Missions," *Missiology* XXXIV, no. 4 (October 2006): 432.

6. See http://www.tlcafrica.com/Liberian_statistics1.htm (accessed October 20, 2015).

7. Governor John Winthrop, "A Model of Christian Charity"

(1630), available from The Winthrop Society, http://winthrop society.com/doc_charity.php (accessed July 15, 2015).

8. See http://www.history.com/topics/monroe-doctrine (accessed July 16, 2015).

9. See http://www.britannica.com/event/Manifest-Destiny (accessed July 7, 2015). The line "from sea to shining sea" in the popular hymn "America the Beautiful" is perhaps the best-known popular expression of Manifest Destiny.

10. Charter of the United Nations, "Chapter 1: Purposes and Principles," www.un.org/en/documents/charter/chapter1.shtml (accessed July 16, 2015).

11. "Major Achievements of the United Nations" at www.un.org/ Overview/achieve.html (accessed July 16, 2015).

12. See http://www.un.org/en/documents/udhr/ (accessed July 23, 2015).

13. Theologians differ on the relationship of the biblical Israel to the modern nation state that bears the same name.

14. See www.brainyquote.com/quotes/quotes/a/abrahamlin388944. html (accessed July 19, 2015).

15. Brian C. Stiller et al., *Evangelicals Around the World: A Global Handbook for the 21st Century* (New York: World Evangelical Alliance, 2015).

16. The well-known anti-corruption agency Transparency International publishes an annual survey assessing the level of corruption in each country. See www.transparency.org/country (accessed July 20, 2015).

17. Sadika Hameed, *The Costs of Corruption: Strategies for Ending a Tax on Private-Sector-Led Growth* (Washington: Center for Strategic International Studies, 2014), v.

18. See http://www.state.gov/j/drl/rls/irf/ and www.uscirf.gov.

19. On nuclear weapons, see the NAE's 2011 resolution, available at www.nae.net.

20. See, for example, David D. Corey and J. Daryl Charles, *The Just War Tradition: An Introduction* (Wilmington, DE: Intercollegiate Studies Institute, 2014).

21. For a detailed discussion of different approaches to war and peace, see the National Association of Evangelicals' 1986 publication on "Peace, Freedom and Security Studies," available at www.nae.net. For a discussion of just peacemaking, see Glen Stassen, *Just Peacemaking: The New Paradigm for the Ethics of Peace and War* (Cleveland: The Pilgrim Press, 2008).

22. Ira Helfand, MD, *Nuclear Famine: Two Billion People at Risk? Global Impacts of Limited Nuclear War on Agriculture, Food Supplies and Human Nutrition*, 2nd ed. (Somerville, MA: International Physicians for the Prevention of Nuclear War, 2013).

23. See www.fews.net.

24. See www.worldrelief.org.

25. See http://foreignpolicy.com/2011/06/20/track-ii-diplomacy-a -short-history/ (accessed July 21, 2015).

CHAPTER 15: CREATION CARE

1. U.S. EPA, "The Benefits and Costs of the CAA, 1970 to 1990: Prepared for U.S. Congress by U.S. Environmental Protection Agency" (October 1997). Report available at http://www.epa .gov/air/sect812/retro.html.

2. U.S. EPA, Office of Air and Radiation, "The Benefits and Costs of the Clean Air Act, 1990 to 2020" (March 2011). Report available at http://www.epa.gov/air/sect812/prospective2.html (accessed August 11, 2015).

3. Cuyahoga River Fire, in Ohio History Central, available at http://www.ohiohistorycentral.org/w/Cuyahoga_River_ Fire?rec=1642 (accessed August 11, 2015).

4. "EPA's 40th Anniversary: 10 Ways EPA has Strengthened

America," available at http://www.aspeninstitute.org/publications/
epa-40th-anniversary-10-ways-epa-has-strengthened-america
(accessed August 11, 2015).

5. Richard Bauckham, *The Bible and Ecology: Rediscovering the Community of Creation* (Waco: Baylor University Press, 2010), 15.

6. "Fauna" in Merrill C. Tenney, gen. ed., *The Zondervan Pictorial Encyclopedia of the Bible*, vol. 2 D-G (Grand Rapids: Zondervan, 1976), 507.

7. See Leviticus 19:18; Matthew 5:43, 19:19, 22:39; Mark 12:31, 33; Luke 10:27; Romans 13:9; Galatians 5:14; James 2:8.

8. National Association of Evangelicals, "Loving the Least of These: Addressing a Changing Environment" (December 2011), available at www.nae.net.

9. Asher Brenner, "Limitations and Challenges of Wastewater Reuse in Israel," in *Clean Soil and Safe Water: NATO Science for Peace and Security, Series C: Environmental Security* (October 3, 2011), 3–9.

10. EPA Fact Sheet: Clean Power Plan and the Role of States (August 2015), available at http://www2.epa.gov/cleanpowerplan/fact-sheet-clean-power-plan-and-role-states (accessed August 15, 2015).

CHAPTER 16: DEALING WITH DIFFERENCES AND DISAGREEMENTS

1. See http://foundationcenter.org/getstarted/faqs/html/howmany.html (accessed July 24, 2015).

2. Available at http://www.thekingcenter.org/archive/document/letter-birmingham-city-jail-0 (accessed August 15, 2015).

3. See www.dictionary.reference.com (accessed July 24, 2015).

4. See http://www.luther.de/en/worms.html (accessed October 20, 2015).

5. See http://www.huffingtonpost.com/2013/10/18/house-democrats-fundraising-september_n_4123208.html (accessed July 24, 2015).

CHAPTER 17: WINNING AND LOSING

1. "Shocking War Crimes in Sierra Leone," Human Rights Watch (June 24, 1999), https://www.hrw.org/news/1999/06/24/shocking-war-crimes-sierra-leone (accessed July 31, 2015).
2. "Treaty of Versailles," *Encyclopedia Britannica* 22 (Chicago: Wm. Benton, 1968), 1000–1004, http://www.britannica.com/event/Treaty-of-Versailles-1919 (accessed July 31, 2015).

CHAPTER 18: A CALL FOR CIVILITY

1. Amy E. Black, "The Cure for Election Madness," in *Christianity Today* (January 2012), 18. (Note: The three who signed were Independent Senator Joseph Lieberman and Republican Representatives Frank Wolf and Sue Myrick. All three have since retired from politics.).
2. Quoted by Donna Leinwand Leger, "Internet creates wider venue for political incivility, threats," in *USA Today* (February 2, 2012), 6A. Susan Herbst is President of the University of Connecticut, a political science professor, and author of *Rude Democracy: Civility and Incivility in American Politics* (Philadelphia: Temple University Press, 2010).
3. Martin Marty, *By Way of Response*, Journey in Faith Series (Nashville: Abingdon Press, 1981), 81.
4. Richard Mouw, *Uncommon Decency: Christian Civility in an Uncivilized World* (Downers Grove, IL: InterVarsity Press, 2010), 14.